HINTS

TO

PERSONS ABOUT BUILDING

IN

THE COUNTRY.

BY A. J. DOWNING,

AUTHOR OF "LANDSCAPE GARDENING," &C., &C.

AND

HINTS TO YOUNG ARCHITECTS.

CALCULATED TO FACILITATE THEIR PRACTICAL OPERATIONS.

BY GEO. WIGHTWICK, Architect

AUTHOR OF "THE PALACE OF ARCHITECTURE," &C.

WITH ADDITIONAL NOTES BY A. J. DOWNING.

Third American Edition.

NEW YORK:
JOHN WILEY, 56 WALKER STREET.
1859.

R. CRAIGHEAD,
Stereotyper and Electrotyper,
Caxton Building,
81, 83, *and* 85 *Centre Street.*

PREFACE

THE HINTS TO YOUNG ARCHITECTS appears to me a volume likely to be of such real and practical assistance to the progress of Domestic Architecture in this country that I have urged its republication here. Mr. WIGHTWICK is one of the most able and spirited English writers in his profession, and his suggestions will, most of them, be equally welcome to young architects in this country.

Besides this, Domestic, or, more especially, Rural Architecture, is now becoming a subject highly interesting to our country gentlemen. By many of the latter, who are constantly interested in building, this volume will be found an exceedingly useful one, particularly in its details and specifications.

To give it, if possible, some additional value, I have added a section of HINTS TO PERSONS ABOUT BUILDING IN THE COUNTRY, which I trust may render the work still more acceptable to many of its readers.

⁂ The notes in the second part which I have added to this edition are designated by [ ].

A. J. D.

Newburgh, N. Y., June, 1847.

HINTS TO PERSONS ABOUT
BUILDING IN THE COUNTRY.

I. WHERE TO BUILD.—II. WHAT TO BUILD.
III. HOW TO BUILD.

Architectural works abound with instructions and illustrations concerning the art of building houses. There are numberless designs for mansions, villas, and cottages in every known style; and there are several eminently useful works, like the present little volume, with minute details for the practical guidance of young architects and artisans.

But we rarely see anything in works on domestic architecture, published in this country, drawing the attention of persons about building, to some very important matters connected with the erection of a dwelling house, which, not to consider properly beforehand, is certain to lead to a great deal of regret, disappointment, and perhaps pecuniary loss.

We allude now to such points as the choice of position, the kind of house best adapted to the wants of the owner, and the proper way to build. These are all matters of the greatest consequence, which really require a great deal of consideration. It is indeed but too common to see persons rushing into all the heavy expenditures of building a large establishment in the country—employing architects, builders, and workmen of all kinds, without any proper knowledge of what they actually want in the accommodations of a house, what are the advantages and disadvantages of various locations, and what kind of dwelling is really best fitted for their habits of life. The inevitable results of all this vagueness of information but too frequently are the selection of unhealthy, bleak, or barren sites, the erection of something tasteless, offensive, or involving double the necessary cost—and the consequences which flow out of these results are but too often many and unavailing regrets of so much expenditure with so little knowledge, or, perhaps, sooner or later, the abandonment of the place at a considerable loss of health and means.

We are very well aware that the safest cure for some of these evils is to employ the best professional services within one's reach, in the shape of an experienced architect. He will both prevent an unnecessary waste of means, and produce much comfort and beauty. But it is not to be denied, that an architect usually has but little to say regarding several important points to which we have alluded. The ground is purchased, the site fixed, and possibly the style of building determined on, in the mind of the proprietor, before the architect's services are requested. And all that remains for him to do is to turn all the existing circumstances, as he finds them, to the best practical account.

Now, since almost every third man in America, living in the country, builds, or may build a house, at some time in his life, it is easy to see how important it is that his attention should be drawn to these preliminary considerations—whether he is afterwards to employ the most celebrated architect in the country, or only the ordinary carpenter of the nearest village in his neighborhood.

Since we are about to write only a *chapter* on this subject, which might very properly occupy a *volume*, we must shape our remarks into something like brevity and conciseness. And we shall therefore throw out a few suggestions touching the points, *where to build, what to build, and how to build.*

I. WHERE TO BUILD.

It very frequently occurs that circumstances compel us to build on a particular site, so that all choice is out of the question. But as there are annually a greater number of new localities selected and built upon in this country, than in any other, this remark applies with less force here than in Europe, and the opportunity of choosing where to build is open to a large majority of those who intend erecting a country dwelling in the United States.

The *best position* for a dwelling house, all other things being equal, it is almost unanimously agreed, is, for an irregular country, a *middle elevation*, half way between the low valleys and the high hills—open to the south and west, and sheltered from the north and east.

The most *popular* sites, those usually chosen by inexperienced proprietors in the middle States, are the summits of hills of moderate elevation, overlooking extensive prospects. Now there are some advantages, but also very great disadvantages, in these high positions. The prominent advantages which such sites are supposed to possess are wide prospects, and conspicuousness for the dwelling itself: *to see*, and *to be seen*, to the greatest possible advantage. But every one having a cultivated taste for fine landscapes, must greatly prefer agreeable views, vistas or portions of trees with rich foregrounds, to wide panoramas of country. It is, in fact, the difference between a pictured landscape, and a geographical map. The *panorama* is striking and interesting, when seen occasionally, but it wants the interest, the home-like feeling of appropriation—which a view of moderate extent affords. As regards the ambition which is gratified with placing one's house where it may be a landmark for ten miles round, it is a false ambition which we have no sympathy with—a taste not in keeping with our social habits, and foreign to that equality of condition which all Americans are impatient of seeing greatly violated. The beauty of a cottage or villa, like all beauty of a higher kind, is, we think, much enhanced by a due concealment, rather than a bold display of its attractions. Gleaming through a veil of soft green foliage, we are led to magnify its charms, from there being something pleasing suggested, which is not seen.

If, on the contrary, we see the whole building studiously exposed, and that but too often in the broad sunshine, we are only inclined to turn away in disappointment.

Besides this, there are practical objections to sites upon the tops of hills, or high ridges, which are of great moment. The first of these is the great difficulty of raising all kinds of trees and shrubs in high and exposed sites. There are, apparently, but few persons aware that ornamental trees will advance twice as rapidly, the soil being the same, in a midway level, or a valley, as they will upon the summits of hills or high ridges. This is partly owing to the high winds, to which they are constantly exposed, and which render the annual growth of wood comparatively dwarfish, and partly to the greater dryness of the soil, which, in this climate, does not afford a continued supply of moisture to the roots. Where a high situation is already sheltered with wood, either of natural growth or artificial plantations, of course this objection regarding slow growth, which cannot be too strongly urged against bare or bald hill sites, is in a great degree removed—for with a good back ground or shelter of wood, any new plantations will be in a great degree protected against the violence of winds.

But we may also add, as an offset to the grand prospect which these elevated sites afford, the labor of walking, riding, or driving up and down a long hill. If the road can be made gradual and easy this is not much, but in situations that we could name, where this is by no means the case, the daily effort (for there is no escape from it) of dragging up and down hill, becomes a burden, to be relieved of which, the proprietor would gladly exchange his wide-spread view for a more limited landscape, and an easier approach. He would be content with a daily view from his windows of moderate extent, and drive or walk to the summit of the hill, once a week, or once a month, for the "grand panorama."

There are many beautiful, tempting, and, we may add, many really excellent sites in *valleys.* The soil is usually fertile, and the growth luxuriant. But the usual objections to narrow and deep valleys, where there is much water, are the dampness, and, often, the unhealthiness, of the air there. Where a valley lies on either side of a running stream which is at all sluggish in its movement, or which either naturally or artificially takes the form of ponds, lakes, or small sheets of shallow water, the atmosphere of the valley is too much charged with moisture to be wholesome after night fall. A single large shallow mill pond, as we have ourselves observed in two instances, is sufficient to cause a slight *malaria* in a narrow valley—and intermittent fevers consequently exist there, when they are entirely unknown 100 rods over the hill side. While, therefore, a wide valley, with a rapid running stream, may be considered as affording perfectly healthy sites for building, a narrow valley, with a sluggish stream, should be avoided by one having it in his power to choose a position for a residence.

There is also another point worthy the consideration of our readers. This is the coldness in winter of all small or deep valleys, compared with the surrounding country. This, though not very perceptible to the senses, exerts a very important influence on vegetation. In a quiet winter night, the coldest air slides down into the bottoms of valleys, while the hills around are in a considerably higher temperature. Hence, many trees and plants will thrive on a higher level, which perish in a deep valley. We know a charming valley in Connecticut, where the peach and the cherry seldom perfect a crop of fruit, owing to the greater severity and prevalence of the frosts there, while they bear uniformly and well, in the adjacent country, on a higher level.

On the other hand, those valleys bordering on large pieces of water, which maintain a more uniform temperature than the land, afford admirable sites for building. Such are the valleys of large rivers and lakes, like the Hudson, and the great lakes in the State of New York. These broad sheets of water have such an effect in equalizing the temperature of the atmosphere for miles around them, that they usually add a month or more to the growing season on their banks. The frosts of Spring and Autumn are warded off, and crops of fruit are preserved, when they are destroyed in the interior of the country. On the banks of a large bay in the Hudson, where we live, the spring is always ten days earlier, and the autumn ten days later, than in the same latitude thirty miles east or west. The shores of lakes Ontario, Erie, and the smaller lakes in this State, which do not freeze in winter, enjoy a still more marked exception from destructive frosts, as compared with the back districts of country unprotected by them. Every person choosing a site for a country residence, who is fond of his garden and orchard, will, therefore, when he has it in his power, give the preference to the borders of large rivers and lakes.

In choosing a position for the house itself, the character of the soil and sub-soil should receive attention. It is evident on a moment's reflection, that the worst soil is one naturally wet, and the best, one naturally dry. The site for a dwelling should never be selected where the sub-soil is naturally wet and springy, unless it is capable of being made perfectly dry by draining—because dampness of the house, and consequent unhealthiness of its inmates, almost inevitably follow the selection of such a situation. A good loam soil, on a gravelly sub-soil, is always an unexceptionable position for placing a house, as far as relates to this point. To those who desire fine ornamental grounds, or even fertile meadows and orchards (and we can hardly imagine the case of any country proprietor who does not), of course, attention to the *quality* of the soil immediately about the site of the house will not be overlooked. Though it is not impossible to render almost any soil fit for cultivation, yet it is infinitely wiser to choose a site where nature has given the necessary conditions of good soil, rather than to undertake the great labor and ill-rewarded expense attending all considerable operations to change the character of soil. Most country gentlemen in America find it a sufficient tax upon their resources to improve, plant, and keep in high order, grounds naturally fertile, without starting with the great additional disadvantage of a bad soil—which is seldom or never thoroughly got rid of. The best soil for all general purposes of culture is a strong loam—the worst, either a very light sand, or a very heavy clay, one being so thin and dry that it requires great quantities of manure, and always parches up in dry weather; and the other is very difficult to work, and is the worst of soils to walk about upon in wet weather. Avoid especially all soils lying upon the tenacious clay sub-soil denominated "*hard pan.*" Without great labor and expense, such soils are very retentive of water, and can never be made satisfactory for tillage.

The *aspect* of the dwelling should be considered in choosing a position. The fixed location of roads, rivers, or other important features in the scene, often lies in the way of a free choice in this particular. At the same time there are numberless instances in which we see great inattention to it, where there was no obstacle to its proper consideration.

The best aspect, in any country, for the principal front of a house, is that towards the *fair weather quarter*—that point of the compass from which the fairest and blandest wind blows most days in the year—and the worst aspect, that from which the greatest number of storms come.

Keeping these principles in view, it is evident that the *south-west* is the best aspect for the dwelling house in the United States, and the *north-east* the worst aspect. The longest, most numerous, and most disagreeable storms come from the last-named point of the compass, and the most delicious of our fair weather days are from what the Indians called the "sweet south-west," the land where their ideal heaven of hunting grounds lies.

A due north aspect is a very objectionable one for a country house, not only on account of the bad weather to which it exposes the principal side of the house, but also because of the accumulation of snow and ice about it in winter, rendering it far more difficult to keep it in hospitable order than a house with a warm southern entrance front.

For a country house which is only intended for summer use, the owner of which leaves it for town in winter, this is not a valid objection. Indeed, a northern entrance is, in our mid-summer, more agreeable, perhaps, than a southern one—its piazzas always cool, and its view opening upon the best and brightest face of the lawn and trees—that turned towards the sun. But the comparatively short season to which this can, in our latitude, be applied with truth, renders a northern aspect a very objectionable one for families residing in the country during the whole year.

In fixing upon a new neighborhood for a country residence, the *health* of that neighborhood is the point of inquiry which should first engage the attention. In some districts of country, otherwise enchanting, intermittent fevers prevail in autumn to such an extent as to become the most insurmountable objection to a residence there. An experienced eye will usually detect the cause in large, low morasses, swamps, or water courses, which become partially dry in summer, and which engender malaria, by exposing a large surface of decaying vegetable matter to the action of a mid-summer sun. We should counsel a friend in search of a site to avoid such localities, though they had otherwise the most seductive charms of scenery, or sylvan accompaniments—and this, more especially, if his family were not robust and strong in health. It is not always easy, even with very straightforward questions, to ascertain the character of a "fever and ague district," though it is well known to the inhabitants. They strive to disguise it from others, and perhaps impose on themselves, very much for the same reason that a man strives to conceal his faults from himself, although they may be notorious to his neighbors.* Besides this, old residents in districts slightly affected by malaria get acclimated, so that they are in a great measure insensible to its effects. But they are none the less dangerous to the new comer, and frequently undermine a slender constitution that would otherwise have endured many years. While, therefore, there is an abundance of wholesome soils in America, with pure air, fine climate, and beautiful scenery, we trust, any one, having it in his power to choose, will avoid districts of this description.

There are some minor considerations which relate to the position of a residence, which we will not follow

* By far the best person of whom to acquire this kind of information is the principal physician of the neighborhood. A reference to his book of cases, and the average of intermittents in August and September, will afford the best proof of the salubrity of the surrounding country.

out in detail here, since their value will be sufficiently apparent to the majority of our readers.

Among these are the advantages and disadvantages of living near towns or villages, the social character of the neighborhood, etc.

To persons of limited income there are evidently manifest advantages in the vicinity of a village, such as the proximity of schools, churches, markets, &c., by which a man of very moderate means may enjoy advantages which would involve considerable additional expenditure in a more distant and scattered neighborhood. The facility of getting and retaining good servants, and the power of using one's legs for short distances, instead of being obliged to use horses and carriages for long ones, are all items worthy of consideration.

In placing the house itself, some thought should also be bestowed on the labor and expense annually involved in a site at a long distance from the public highway. There is nothing more agreeable than a long approach, well kept, through an extensive reach of lawn, wood, pleasure ground, or even meadow and orchard landscape. But there are but few persons who "calculate" in the outset the annual cost of keeping up half a mile or a mile of gravel roads and walks, and unless they are, or can be kept, in proper condition, we should by all means advise placing the dwelling nearer the road, so that the private entrance, at least, shall not wear a slovenly and neglected air, from the want of means to keep it in scrupulously neat order.

II. WHAT TO BUILD.

Almost all persons, on the first consideration of the subject of building, when the question arises what *style* of dwelling shall be erected, answer it directly by saying, "Oh, that is a mere matter of taste—you may prefer one style, B another, and C a third; I like this style, and no other will suit me."

We do not forget the old proverb—*de gustibus non est disputandum.* It is well enough to allow ignorant and prejudiced men such an excuse for their peculiarities of character, which they have not wit enough to analyse or account for. But, in the main, the maxim is entirely unphilosophical and untrue. Mere personal tastes—by which is meant a capricious preference of any one mode of producing a certain effect, may be strongly disputed, and the reasons why certain modifications of art are best fitted for certain places or purposes very distinctly proved.

The philosophical principles which govern, or ought to govern, reasoning beings in the selection of any style of architecture for a dwelling, are those of *fitness* and *propriety.* They are principles which no correct artist, or reflecting person, can violate, or does violate strongly, without raising discordant, instead of harmonious and satisfactory emotions in the minds of all lovers of art, as well as all lovers of common sense—the world-constituted judges of the *Beautiful* and the *True.*

There is, indeed, perhaps, no legal or moral reason why a man should not indulge his taste (by which, indeed, is usually meant his caprice or *fancy*) in a dwelling-house in any known style, from the Pawnee wigwam of bark and skins, to the pagoda of a Chinese mandarin, with curved roof and pendent bells.

Neither is there any better reason why he should not dress himself in the oriental costume of a Mussulman, with turban and flowing trowsers, or that of an independent Tartar Chief with high cap and long jacket. These are forcible and picturesque styles, as truly appropriate in our streets and social life, as houses are, built in the Chinese taste, or domestic copies of Egyptian temples—the latter with their unchristian ornaments "of embalmed cats and deified crocodiles."

It does not require any argument to prove that it is this feeling of a violation of the principles of fitness and propriety which prevents men from adopting foreign and grotesque styles of dress. An enlightened society would demand good reasons from an individual of its number who should carry his principle of *not having his taste disputed* to its whole length and breadth. A naturalized Turk or Arab, settled among us, might perhaps justify himself on the ground of long habit and hereditary custom, brought from a country where there was fitness in it; but not a native born citizen. It is not in "good taste," as the world say, and say correctly, because there is no significance or meaning in it.

We conceive it to be true that the same principle should govern us in the choice of a style for a dwelling-house. Although we would reject no foreign style because it is foreign, we would adopt nothing in our domestic architecture which has not some obvious beauty of purpose, or some significance for our country and climate—which has not, in short, that fitness and propriety which a refined and just taste can fully approve.

This would lead us to reject at once all styles of building belonging to barbarous and semi-civilized people, as too grotesque in effect, and too much at variance with our habits of life, to be a significant and true expression of our age and social life. It would confine our choice to what may properly be called European styles—such as Gothic, Grecian, Roman, Italian, Swiss; or to new and more suitable modifications of these styles. A country of the variety of climate and geographical breadth of ours, indeed demands a like variety of style in its domestic architecture. In the houses of the north, warmth and shelter are the first requisites, and the comfortable dwellings of England and the north of Europe may be studied to advantage. In those of the south the cool verandas and the spacious colonnades of Italian architecture will be most appropriate and significant. One of the leading rules in selecting plans for a dwelling, which we deduce from the principles of fitness and propriety, is that of abjuring all styles or modifications of styles not warranted by our social and domestic habits.

It is one of the most common errors into which persons fall, whose architectural taste is just awakening, to rush to the very verge and extreme limits of architectural style. Not content with simplicity, or a moderate degree of ornament, everything they do must have a "strong relish" about it. If they are about to build Gothic, it must be an imitation of a castle of the middle ages at least; if Grecian, nothing short of a copy of the Parthenon will satisfy them. Now there is little meaning, to our eyes, in the mock heroic air of a puny Gothic castle built in a style which was warranted by feudal times and feudal robberies, for the habitation by a meek and quiet merchant, who has not the remotest idea of manifesting anything offensive or defensive to any of his peace-loving neighborhood. And we cannot greatly admire the effect of a huge Greek colonnade round four sides of the house, supported on columns two stories high, affording little shade or shelter, and costing half the entire sum that ought to have been expended in the dwelling itself.

It is the *later* modifications of European architecture which ought to be studied and adopted by our architects, and persons about building, at the present time. These are based upon modern comforts, and modern wants, and their beauty is the more beautiful that it grows out of, and is in keeping with, the spirit of utility. Hence the Tudor or Elizabethan villa, and the Rural English cottage, are the varieties of the Gothic style which may be copied with more propriety in this country. For the same reason the Roman style is preferable to the Greek, and the modern Italian, in its many variations, to the Roman itself. Significance, fitness, propriety, immediately lead us to ask for verandas, piazzas, porches, balconies, clustered chimneys, window-blinds, and all the numerous architectural features that denote refined comforts and the enjoyments of our social life. Since these do not belong, and cannot with propriety be attached to the old Gothic castle and Greek temple, let us eschew these latter, and take some more pliant and appropriate style of which they properly form a part.*

It is difficult also for a tyro in architecture, as well indeed as in other arts, to perceive, amid the glitter of ornament, the superior dignity and beauty of *simplicity.* Hence, we see the principles we have stated, continually violated, by those who are striving after an excess of ornament, or decoration, in their dwelling-houses. We confess as hearty a love of decoration and ornament in architecture as any one. But it must be *consistent,* to satisfy us. It must express a beauty which pervades the building itself, everywhere, and not seem *patched on,* to catch the eye, and hide its defects. Harmonious proportions, a well ordered distribution of parts, excellent construction, and, *afterwards,* a suitable degree of decorations. Else it is like a poor book badly printed, yet richly bound and glittering with gold leaf.

The practical rule which we would deduce from this may be briefly enough stated. Attempt no ambitious imitations of a certain style, which you have not the *means of carrying out.* If your wealth permit you to build a villa throughout in an enriched style, do not

* Individual habits and hereditary descent, when they are sufficiently marked, may give a certain fitness to a given style of architecture. We could mention a gentleman of large possessions in this country, who is descended from an old Dutch family, and who has lately built a magnificent country residence in the Anglo-Italian style. We never see it without thinking how much additional fitness and propriety he might have conferred on his estate by building a fine specimen of the old Dutch or Flemish mansion, and making it a family museum of the superb specimens of Dutch furniture and interior decoration which were still within his reach.

hesitate to give the public an example of beauty and fine taste. But do not endeavor to give a cheap cottage the air of an enriched villa, by a few carvings and showy ornaments on the exterior, when you are obliged to make the interior meagre and poor. A cottage, admirably planned, and tastefully built, so that every part bears the impress of refined judgment and selection, is capable of giving quite as much pleasure in its way as a spacious mansion. It is not, of course, the same kind of pleasure, but it will be perfect of its kind—while, if, in the modest dimensions of the cottage, we see an ambitious striving after the decoration and style of enrichment that belong to the mansion, it destroys all the beauty of truthfulness and propriety.

Indeed harmony of form, what is commonly called *good proportion*, is a much more genuine and enduring source of pleasure than decoration—by which we mean, of course, ornaments applied to the surface of a building to add to its effect. An edifice in a simple style, admirably proportioned, cannot fail to please every one. The richest and most florid specimen of domestic architecture, if its proportions are not good, fails to please any but vulgar minds; and the pleasure which the cultivated taste derives from elaborate decoration is of a description far less strong and enduring than that bestowed by harmonious proportions, and a refined and chaste simplicity.

We might add a few words here touching the relation which the character of the dwelling in the country ought to bear to its site—under the action of this principle. It is not an uncommon spectacle to see a country house built at a lavish expenditure, and in a very ornate style, but placed in the midst of grounds badly laid out and wretchedly kept. The proprietor has exhausted all his forced stock of enthusiasm, and spent all his surplus capital upon his villa, in his architectural *fever*, and his grounds are doomed to suffer the succeeding *ague* of indifference and neglect. A wise man, when he plans a country residence, will so apportion his means that his house may not be out of keeping with his grounds. The same style, the same feeling, should pervade both, and be reflected from one to the other. Indeed we would counsel our countrymen to follow the English in this respect, who, with their usual good taste, let the pleasure grounds outshine the house, or rather, render simple cottages pictures of rural beauty by the profusion of blossoming trees, shrubs, and vines, with which they embower and clothe them.

To assist us in determining *what to build*, the character of the scenery itself should be considered. There is a fitness which natural construction and long association have bestowed on certain styles, as connected with particular kinds of landscape. Thus the Rural English cottage in fertile valleys; the Swiss cottage on the sides, or under the brow of steep mountains; the abbey and the villa in smiling plains; and the castle in bold rocky passes.*

* We could name a monstrous architectural absurdity in a neighboring State, in the shape of a large country residence, built in imitation of an old castle, with towers and battlements, *all of wood!* To render this specimen of folly and bad taste more glaring, the proprietor selected for its site the smooth green

The simplest rule for determining what style of building is best adapted to a particular kind of scenery, is to determine first the character of both the architecture and the landscape in question. Our own maxim is, that the bolder and more irregular the scenery, the bolder and more irregular the style of architecture it demands. Hence, buildings with highly varied outlines, with towers and the like, are most fittingly placed amid bold hills, and in a broken and mountainous country.

For a flat or level country, almost any simple style of building is in good keeping. Hence the propriety of the modifications of the cottage and villa forms which generally prevail there, and which are always pleasing when they express the simple life of the country gentleman, farmer, or proprietor of the soil—and equally unpleasing when they exhibit the finery of town houses, or ambitious architectural ornaments not properly answering to the habits or wants of their inhabitants.

In determining what to build, a few brief hints may be worthy of a place here respecting practical points that are worthy the attention of the proprietor. Among these the *form* of the house itself is an important one.

All builders will agree that the most economical form in which a dwelling can be erected is a *cube*, because it

banks of one of the tamest rivers, in the flattest district in America, where the only warfare carried on is against oysters and woodcock! A man of imagination and wealth might be pardoned for building up, from the massive primitive rock, an imitation of a grand old Rhine castle on the top of one of the bold hills in the Hudson Highlands. One would, perhaps, from the keeping between the striking scenery and the edifice, find it difficult to believe that it did not actually belong to the past. But a wooden castle, in a flat meadow, is as much out of place as a knight in armor would be running a tilt in the Jersey pine barrens contains more space within a given area of walls and roof than any other. Next to this is a parallelogram. The more irregular the outline of a building, the more the cost is increased, because it has more exterior surface, and therefore requires more wall or weather boarding, more roof, more gutters, and more fixtures and ornaments, when the house is in a handsome style.*

On the other hand, the irregular form has great advantages, not only in the greater beauty of effect which the architect is enabled to bestow on it, but in its greater variety of sizes, forms, and consequently accommodation of its apartments within, as well as in the greater number and variety of views afforded without.

Hence, those who desire to combine as much economy as possible, with good taste in building a residence, will select a cube or rectangle for the outline of its ground plan; while those to whom expense is of less importance than convenience and picturesque effect, will adopt the irregular form.

Viewing the different styles of building with regard to the economy of first cost, and as well as after expenditure in repairs, we may add that, for this climate, all styles, or modifications of styles, with broad *projecting* roofs, are greatly to be preferred. These projecting roofs not only shelter the building in summer against heat, but they protect it in the most effectual manner against the violent storms, ever changing from snow to rain, of our northern winters. The difficulty and expense of keep-

* The most agreeable cottages and villas in the form of a cube that we recall to mind, are those pretty specimens in Hillhouse avenue, New Haven.

ing a roof in order, with the flush parapet of the Tudor, or the moulded cornice of the Grecian style, is double or treble as great as that in the Italian or Swiss mode of building—because, in the former style, in case of any defect, overflow, or leakage in the gutters, all the water is carried by the projecting eaves far beyond the walls of the house; while in the latter it runs down the face of the wall, or, what is worse, finds its way into the interior of the house. Hence it is sufficiently evident, that the outer walls of a house, when they are of brick, stucco, or wood, will last twice as long, and require only half the repairs, under a roof that projects two feet or more, than under such a roof as is usually built in a common dwelling in any modification of the Grecian style. Those, therefore, who undertake to build with valley and parapet gutters, should be willing also to incur the cost of the very best materials and workmanship, for any other would soon require to be repaired or renewed altogether.*

Of what *materials* to build is one of the first questions to be settled when the site of the house has been determined upon. In some parts of the country, indeed, the abundance and cheapness of one material, and the scarceness and high cost of others, renders it imperative

* Among the growing fashions in building which we think seriously objectionable in this climate, are French *casement* windows where they are exposed to the weather. Under piazzas, or verandas, where they are protected, they are there often well and properly introduced. But as it is nearly or quite impossible to make them wind and water tight in exposed situations, we strongly advise the use of the common rising sash instead. We never knew an instance where they were largely introduced into a country house without great after-regret on the part of its owner.

upon the majority to employ that which is most easily obtained. A large part of the United States is still in this condition with regard to *wood*, which, especially in the newer States, is still so abundant as to be much the cheapest building material. When it is necessary to build of wood, our advice is always to choose a style which is rather light, than heavy—in other words, one in which the style and material are in keeping with each other. It is in false taste to erect a wooden building in a massive and heavy style, which originated in the use of stone, as it would be senseless to build a mock fortification, intended to stand a real siege, whose walls and battlements are of thin pine boards.

In the Atlantic States, however, a large portion of the better class of houses, erected within the last five years, are of rough hard brick, covered on the exterior with a coat of cement. This affords on the whole, perhaps, the dryest and warmest house in winter, and the coolest in summer, at a very moderate cost, that can be built. The art of stucco work, or cement plastering the exterior of the walls, formerly so badly performed, is now becoming well understood, and when well done (and more especially when protected by a projecting roof) it will last without repairs for twenty or thirty years. On this account it is also greatly preferable to wood, which requires painting every third or fourth year to preserve it from decay. Any pleasing neutral stone tint may be given to stucco, and thus all the effect of handsome dressed stone obtained at one fourth its cost. There is no doubt that, from its many advantages, brick-and stucco is destined to become the prevalent mode of building the better class of our country houses.

Where stone of an agreeable color can be obtained, we do not hesitate to give the preference to it. It makes the most solid, substantial, and enduring house, and there is, perhaps, a look of permanence about a fine stone mansion which no other material ever has. But we would decidedly prefer brick-and-stucco, for a cottage or dwelling of moderate size, to stone of a cold and gloomy color—such as dark blue limestone or dark granite. The expression of a cottage or villa of moderate size in the country, should, by all means, be that of cheerfulness, and, when built of a dark stone, it can scarcely fail to be the opposite. Only in a large mansion do we think a dark stone can be happily employed for a dwelling-house—since there it often adds to the grandeur and dignity of effect. Some of our lighter freestones, like that of Trinity Chuch, New York, and that so much used at Cincinnati, are beautiful building materials, which cannot be too much or too frequently used.*

* There is a strong prejudice, we find, in the Eastern States against stone houses, which we think entirely erroneous, and which undoubtedly retards the progress of domestic architecture—for it is undoubtedly true that this art advances in proportion as the materials employed possess solidity and permanence. This prejudice has arisen from the bad manner in which the old stone houses of that part of the country were all constructed. There were two errors in their construction: 1st, the foundation walls were often laid in damp or springy soil, with common lime mortar; 2d, the interior walls were plastered on the solid walls of the house without *firring*. Now it is impossible that a house built in this way should be dry. The moisture of the soil is absorbed by the foundation walls, and is carried up, by capillary attraction, often as high as the second story, and the dampness which the outer walls themselves absorb in long storms passes through, more or less, to the walls of the rooms. To prevent the

III. HOW TO BUILD.

Most men in America, who build country houses, are their own "Clerk of the Works," that is to say, they undertake to supply the materials, and employ the mechanics; they mostly plan the building, and they take all the general superintendence of the labor. And a sorry time they have of it! If it strengthens patriotism to fight battles for one's country, our amateur builders ought to have a patriotic attachment to their country homes, for many of them have a sore conflict of mind and body from the time they commence building till they bid a joyful adieu to the house-painter.

It does not require much observation to discover the reason of all this difficulty and perplexity. To state it plainly, it is nothing more nor less than the ignorance of the proprietor himself of the whole art of building. Every man does not fancy that he can make a coat, or weave Gobelin tapestry, without instruction—yet every man is quite certain, *till he has tried*, that he can not only build a house, but build a much better one, in many respects, than he has seen before!

He commences by planning, with the assistance perhaps of his carpenter, the proposed dwelling. After

former evil it is only necessary to lay the foundation walls with a mortar composed of cement, or water-lime, and sand, instead of common lime and sand—this effectually prevents all dampness being absorbed or conducted up from the soil itself. To prevent all dampness finding its way from the outside to the inner walls of the rooms, what is technically called "firring off," that is, making a hollow space between the lathing and the outer wall, is a most effectual and simple remedy some little perplexities in the arrangements of doors, windows, and chimneys, which will not come as easily in their proper places as he conceived they would—after a rough draft of specifications, and the selection of the site, the building is commenced.

No sooner is the first floor timbered, and the skeleton of the house erected, than he discovers some very important oversight—some additional room which it is impossible to do without, or a couple of windows which are truly indispensable. A set of closets have been wholly overlooked, which the mistress of the villa declares absolutely necessary to her existence, and since the building has been in progress, a visit to some new house in the neighborhood has revealed the incomparable value of a *back-stairs*. All these, by some means or other, must either be appended or "dove-tailed" into the house. Timbers are laid aside, partitions are taken down, and half the work already done is sacrificed, because the proprietor did not really know what he desired in a dwelling before he commenced. If he is building by contract, the contractor is glad of the opportunity to double his profits by extra charges for work, when there is now no competitor to lower his prices. If he is building by day's work, the mechanics are not anxious to hurry forward with their work, when it is likely enough it may be half pulled down for a new improvement next month.

Then, again, our amateur builder is no judge of materials. When his interior walls begin to dry, he finds them cracking from the shrinking of sappy or unseasoned wood which has been mixed with the good timber, and employed without his detecting the faulty material. He has contracted with the head workmen for the whole of the work according to his specifications. But he is not a little surprised, almost every week, while the building is going forward, by a demand from the carpenter, bricklayers, or others engaged in the work, for many articles of vital importance which "are not in the contract," which they are therefore not bound to furnish, and which go of course to swell the bill of *extras.*

The most effectual way of avoiding all this disappointment and perplexity, where a dwelling of any importance is to be built, is to put the whole, at the outset, into the hands of some *architect* of acknowledged ability—let him satisfy you, in the commencement, with the plans, and then contract with him to complete the house in a certain style and finish. He will charge you from 7 to 10 per cent. on the whole cost of the building, and will, if he is a man of ability and integrity, give you a good specimen of architectural style, and a comfortable, convenient, and well finished house. If you undertake to be architect and master-builder yourself, it will cost you at least 20 *per cent.*, and it is most likely you will produce a building that your neighbors will compassionate you for being obliged to live in, and that is full of real inconveniences.

Another course, less complete, but by which many beautiful houses are every day erected, is that of employing the best architectural talent to design and furnish the working drawings, and specifications complete (at a charge usually of 5 per cent. on the cost of the house), and then contract with the best master-builder, within your reach, to carry the whole into execution.*

There are but few men, inexperienced in building, who can understand that there is as much *economy* in employing the best professional talent in planning and erecting a house, as in conducting a lawsuit. But the fact is demonstrated every day in the year, and the experimental knowledge of it is purchased at almost too dear a rate for us not to desire to warn the novice against attempting it over again.

When circumstances render it difficult or impossible to employ an architect, endeavor to avoid the difficulties we have pointed out, by studying every part of your plans very thoroughly before you commence building. If you are not familiar with all the details of the house you propose to build, make yourself so, by a repeated examination of existing specimens, in dwellings in the same style, already erected. Above all, do not be satisfied by the mere expression on the plan, in figures, of the sizes of your rooms; but ascertain if the size is exactly what you suppose, and what you want, by looking at rooms already built of that size. Otherwise you may find to your regret, when it is too late, that "parlor 16 by 20"

* We ought, perhaps, in strict justice to remark, *en passant*, that every one who calls himself an *architect* in our cities, is by no means entitled to that appellation. Some are mere builders of "three story bricks," and others have assumed the title and commenced business with only a knowledge of the rudiments of their art. The safest way, after all, to arrive at a knowledge of what a man can do, is to see what he has done. Before you employ an architect, therefore, of whose abilities you are ignorant, examine thoroughly a dwelling-house that he has built, and you will soon discover his merits or defects, to which knowledge the owner will probably assist you.

means something a great deal smaller, when actually enclosed within four walls, than it did in the air castle of your imagination, which you conjured up with the aid of your paper plans.

Not to be disappointed in the cost of your house, it is only necessary that the *specifications* should be full and perfect. This is the weak point with most builders, and it is the unguarded loop-hole whence all the *fearful extras* find admittance. It is the main purpose of the following "Hints to Young Architects," to suggest specifications that might be overlooked, and of which, with the assistance of your master mechanics, you can also avail yourself. If, also, you have a neighbor, who has already "bought his experience" in the same way you are about to do, and has noted down the short-comings in his own specifications, his notes will be a valuable assistance to you in enabling you to avoid the same costly shoals.

We have throughout spoken of building *by contract*, because a good deal of observation and experience has convinced us that this is, in nearly all cases, the better mode in this country. If your master-workman is a man of integrity, he will serve you as faithfully under a fair contract as by the day's-work system, and, if he is not, there is even more likelihood of your being cheated in the latter case than in the former. Letting the work under contract, makes the contractor the only accountable person, and your own supervision is confined to observing that he fulfils the conditions of his contract;

and rids you, besides, of the trouble of watching a dozen or twenty subordinates.

There is an opinion strongly maintained by some (and for the indulgence of which they are willing to pay dearly), that good workmanship can only come by the *day's-work* system. We have not found, on comparison of houses built in the different modes, that there is any practical truth in it. Everything, as we have said, depends on the master-workman, and, in this country, if he is allowed a fair compensation for the "job," we believe as much justice is always done in one case as the other.

One thing is undoubtedly true—that in building a house, there is a great deal of *rough work* which must be done, and which, if done by contract, can be as well done by apprentices and inferior workmen, as by the most accomplished mechanics. A contractor, with a large set of hands, is thus enabled to do with much economy what would be done at the highest cost, and an unnecessary expense by the day's-work mode.

It should not be forgotten, however, that in letting out a building by contract, the proposals of the lowest offering party should by no means be invariably accepted. A preference of a few hundred dollars will frequently secure you a faithful contractor, who will truly fulfil his engagement in the spirit, as well as the letter; while the lowest bid, tempting though it may appear, if accepted, would involve an increased after-expense. In other words, endeavor to make a fair contract, with a safe and responsible master-workman, whose integrity and abilities are known, rather than accept the offer of a builder whose capacity is not so well established, and whose offer is so much below the others, as to lead you to doubt if he can do himself justice in taking the contract, without injuring your interests.

Above all, do not forget that everything which originally enters into your estimate, through previous forethought and careful study of your real wants, and the expression of them in your plans and specifications, will cost you *about half as much*, taken in the whole contract, as it will do if it is an after-thought, and is introduced as an improvement, or alteration, when the house is fairly in progress.

A. J. D

[*We subjoin, as a guide, an outline sketch of Specifications, form of Contract, &c., as generally employed in the United States. The details must of course be filled up and varied to suit the building to be erected.*]

SPECIFICATIONS

OF THE MATERIALS AND WORKS NECESSARY IN BUILDING THE BRICK AND CEMENT DWELLING HOUSE FOR OF ACCORDING TO THE ACCOMPANYING PLANS, ELEVATIONS, AND SECTIONS ANNEXED, AND THE CONDITIONS SUBJOINED.

These plans, &c., referred to herein, are numbered as follows, and consist of:

No. I. Basement and foundations.
II. Plan of the principal story.
III. Plan of the second story
IV. Attic and roof.
V. Elevation of the principal front.
VI. Elevation of the rear.
VII. Longitudinal section.
VIII. Transverse section.

[Also insert the number of such working drawings as are necessary.]

⁂ These drawings, and such figures, writing, and details as may be upon them, are to be considered as part of, and as illustrating, these specifications. In the plans, *blue* designates stone; *red*, brick; and *yellow*, wood

MASON AND BRICKLAYER.

Excavate the ground for the basement or cellars according to the area of the plan, and to the depth requisite to bring the level of the principal floor feet above the average natural level of the earth.

Remove from time to time all soil, rocks, and stones from such excavations not wanted there, and all rubbish that accumulates about and in the building—the same to be carried to such place as may be agreed upon before entering into the contract.

Dig trenches for the foundation walls 2 feet lower than the level of the basement or cellar floors. Dig trenches for the footings of all piers and areas 3½ feet deep, and of the requisite width. Dig foundation for cistern.

LIME AND MORTAR.—Provide a shed for all lime used, to prevent its injury by exposure. The mortar used shall be made in the best manner, of the best [Thomaston] lime, sharp sand, and fresh water, using not less than one part lime to two parts sand.

[N.B.—If the soil is damp, specify that the foundation walls shall be laid with hydraulic cement mortar instead of common lime mortar.]

FOUNDATIONS AND CELLAR WALLS.—Lay the foundations with large stone, flat bedded, and of nearly equal thickness. The walls to be carried up to the water table of the thickness marked in the plans, and with offsets on each side of 6 inches, as per sections. After the work is seasoned, fill-in, and well ram the earth around the walls.

Build cellar partition of good hard brick as per plans.

Build stone foundations for the SINK; with a brick drain of laid in hydraulic cement [or hollow tiles] feet long, and inches in the clear inside. Fit to the drain, to prevent rising of smells, one or more cast iron dip-traps, 8 inches square. Build area walls, inches thick, in front of the basement window of stone. Pave the same with brick, and if the soil is retentive, provide small drains to convey the water into the main drain.

Steps.—The steps are to be laid of granite, marble, free-stone, or blue-stone, as marked upon the plan, and of the number and dimension upon the same.

Water Table.—Provide and set in the best manner, a water table, or plinth, of stone, quite round the building. The stones of the same to be not less than three feet long, to be thoroughly secured in the wall, and the joints to be run with lead; the water table to be bevelled on the upper outer edge sufficiently to throw off the water, and to project inches beyond the outer face of the wall.

Sills and Lintels.—Provide and set stone sills to all the doors and windows (10 inches wide and in one stone) of the form and dimensions in the plans; all those, except for the basement, being worked, tooled, and finished in the best manner. The lintels to be plain, bevelled, or moulded, as per working drawings and plans. Provide and set in their proper places all cornices, mouldings, or caps of stone, as per elevations.

Oven.—Build a brick oven 3 ft. by 3½ ft., clear interior measure, upon suitable foundations. Provide and fix the best patent door and frame complete for the same.

Paving and Flagging.—Pave the cellar or basement floors so marked on the plans, with the best hard pressed paving brick. The cellars marked pave with common stock brick [or lay with square blue flag-stone]. Those marked are to be furnished with mortar floors. The whole to be duly levelled, and also drained where necessary.

The entire masonry, and all joints, mouldings, drips, sinkings, &c., are to be bedded and set in the very best manner, and, wherever necessary, to have stone and lead plugs, and copper or iron cramps. All horizontal mouldings and projections to be wrought with joggled water joints, which are to be run with lead [or grouted with hydraulic cement]. All grooves, jointings, rebates, &c., to be well cut and fitted, and proper bond stones to be worked-in, to make sound and strong walls. The needful wooden bricks and strips to be furnished by the carpenter are to be worked-in as the walls are laid up.

Cistern.—Build where directed a rain-water cistern, that will contain hogsheads; the walls of 8 inch hard brick, arched and cemented so as to be perfectly tight on the inside. To be provided with an opening in the top, 2 feet square, and with the apertures for the necessary pipes. Build also a waste drain of to carry off the overflow.

Brickwork.—All the bricks used in the walls to be good, hard, well-burned bricks. They must be laid wet, with flushed solid joints, leaving no interstices or empty spaces in the walls. As the walls are to be plastered or cemented on the outside, the joints should not be pointed, but raked out, or left rough.

All the outer and main walls of the building, from the water table to the roof, to be inches thick. These walls on the centres of basement walls so as to leave a projection of inches to face of the water-table.

[Hollow brick walls are preferred by many as cheaper and dryer than solid ones. When hollow walls are built, firring-off is not necessary.]

Build brick discharging arches, to take the weight of walls from the lintels over all doors and windo openings of the walls. Strong brick inverted arche to be turned under all the principal openings. Turn trimmer arches to support all hearth stones.

The brickwork shall be well bedded and flushed up, tied in every course, and worked in sound and regular bond. Fill-in and back-close with sound bricks and good mortar, at the back of all ashlaring or facing stone work, and *point-up-home* to all sills, copings, casings, and projections. Bed carefully and solidly all window and door frames, and underpin all sills with suitable mortar. Provide the needful materials of every description, and cover the work from the weather at all necessary times; find all the scaffolding necessary for the performance of the work, and remove the same when the work is completed. Attend the other mechanics when required to back-in and fill up properly behind their work. Fill-in all the angles between wall plate and roof, and all spaces in the walls between the ends of the beams. Also all wooden partitions (if any are used). The walls shall be carried up and built in a substantial, workman-like manner, and no part shall be carried up more than four feet faster than another, except gables or chimney shafts.

Stuccoing.—After the outer walls have become well seasoned, the stucco or cement shall be put upon it [not later in the season than the month of September]. Previously to stuccoing, the outer walls shall be thoroughly wetted and scrubbed clean with a broom. The cement composed of sharp pit or river sand, washed perfectly clean, and the best hydraulic lime [that from Berlin, Ct., is most excellent], shall be mixed only as fast as it can be used and finished off at once in two coats only. The whole to be marked off in courses and tinted in imitation of stone.

[If in water colors, it should be done immediately; if in oil, not till the work is perfectly dry.]

FIREPLACE in kitchen and   to have lintels, and hearths, and jambs of   stone, of ample size and strongly set. Openings of fire places of all rooms in the principal and second stories to be   feet high by   feet wide; that in kitchen   feet by   feet; that in wash-room   feet by   feet.

Prepare all fire places in first and second stories for marble mantels, and set the same in the best manner; which mantels shall be selected [or furnished] by the proprietor.

Kitchen flue to be 14 inches in the clear; and other flues to be   inches in the clear, and well plastered or pargetted in the inside. Iron chimney bars, ½ by 2½ inches, to be set where needed. Flues to be gathered in above the fire-place in such a manner as to secure a good draught, and in all cases separate flues to be carried up from each fire-place. Build chimney tops of brick [or set those of cut stone] to correspond with the drawings. Set all grates, ranges, and stoves, required for the several fire-places, using fire-brick facings.

DEAFEN OR PUG with a layer of good pugging mortar, 2 inches thick, all floors throughout the house; finishing the same with a coat of lime and hair mortar flush up to the flooring.

LATH AND PLASTER the kitchen and   rooms, and finish the same with brown walls. Lath and plaster and finish with three coats [hard finish] all rooms, closets, and partitions, in the first and second stories. [The first coat is called the *scratch coat;* the second, the *brown coat;* the third, *hard finish.* Diagonal lathing is greatly to be preferred in all cases where the timber is likely to shrink, as it lessens the risk of cracks in the walls.]

Run all cornices, and fix all stucco ornaments in the ceilings of the different apartments to correspond exactly with models and patterns fixed and agreed upon before signing the contract.

The contractor for the foregoing, including all masonry, stone-cutting, bricklaying, plastering, and labor and carriage pertaining thereto, shall find all the necessary materials of every description, tools, tackle, iron work, boards, horses or tressels, moulds, ladders, &c., for the performance of his work ; and to do the whole in the best and most workmanlike manner, subject to the conditions at the end of the specifications.

CARPENTER AND JOINER.

All the wood and timber used in this building shall be of the best White Pine [except where otherwise specified] perfectly well seasoned, and free from loose or dead knots, sappy parts, shakes, or other defects. The Carpenter shall frame and construct according to the drawings and sections, and in the best and most workmanlike manner, all parts of the wood work ; fix strongly all requisite straps, stirrups, and other irons ; and allow no joists rafters, quarters, or battenings, to be more than inches apart.

Roof.—Frame the roof as per plan and sections, so as to make a strong and substantial frame ; the rafters place 2 feet 6 inches apart. Frame King posts of into every third pair of rafters, and secure the same with iron straps. The Wall plates shall be , and must be halved and spiked together at every angle.

Construct a *skylight*, glazed in the best manner of thick crown glass, , over the ; and a scuttle door in the roof over ; both to be made water tight in all parts.

Cover the roof with the best shingles [or slates], laying no shingles [or slates] upon the valleys until the latter are thoroughly laid with copper. The whole to be laid in the best manner and repaired, if necessary, when leaks are found, till it is perfectly water tight. [If the roof is to be covered with tin or zinc, specify the quality and the mode of fixing the metal, whether ridged and lapped, or soldered.]

BASEMENT STORY.—Floors of sound inch yellow pine plank, inches wide, tongued and grooved, to be laid in the kitchen and rooms in this story, on sound oak sleepers.

Doors.—The doors to the kitchen and rooms to be 1½ inches thick, 4 panel doors, hung with strong butt hinges, and fitted with brass inch knob-locks, of good quality. The doors in cellars to be 1¼ inch thick, and fitted with neat iron latches and iron bolts. The outward basement door to be 2 inch, 6 panel, made flush and fitted with a strong inch iron mortice lock and an iron bolt.

Windows.—Windows in kitchen to be rising sash windows, in box frames, with lights by ; windows in rooms to be the same, lights by . Cellar windows to be , and provided with gratings securely fitted.

Shutters to be made to all the windows in the basement story of 1½ inch white pine, with panels, hung to open side, and provided with proper fastenings for the outside and inside.

Bases of inch stuff, inches high, to be made in kitchen and rooms.

Stairs.—Build stairs from basement to principal story ft. wide, with risers inches, and treads inches. The latter of best Southern yellow pine. Fit a plain mahogany hand rail to the same. Fit up the sink complete, ready for the plumber.

PRINCIPAL STORY.—Floors.—Beams to be of and inches by inches, and to be laid not over inches apart from centre to centre, with the necessary trimmers and trimmer beams; the former to be framed in at all the fire-places, stairs, in both stories. All beams to rest on the walls at least 6 inches; to have two tiers of bracings, of $1\frac{1}{4}$ plank, 9 inches deep, and prepared for deafening throughout. Floors to be laid of the best quality, $1\frac{1}{8}$ inch tongued and grooved plank only 6 inches wide, and to be blind nailed. Hearth borders to be made to all fire places in this and second story.

Partitions.—Those partitions marked yellow on plan, and not built of brick, are to be made of studs, by inches, placed inches apart. Double studs shall be introduced at the door jambs; and wide partitions, or those not resting over solid walls, shall be well braced with *diagonal* braces.

Doors.—Front or entrance door to be of 2 inch clear white pine, panelled as per drawing, hung with inch butts, and furnished with a inch mortice lock of the best quality. Casing with mouldings and side lights, as per plan and drawings annexed. All other doors in this story to be 2 inch panel doors as per working drawings, made of perfectly seasoned white pine [mahogany, black walnut ?], and hung with butts, and fitted with inch mortice locks, with brass [silver plated, enamel ?] furniture worth each. Sills of these doors to be of . The doors to closets in dining room to be .

Windows.—All windows in this story to be of the sizes and dimensions as per plans, with box casings of pine, fitted with sills and sliding pieces of ; hung complete with double weights, best pulleys, &c. The sashes to be double sliding sashes, inches thick, with each lights by inch. [Except windows in room, which are to be casement windows opening to the floor, with lights by inches.] All windows to be provided with strong and neat locks worth each.

Shutters.—The walls to be firred-off to a sufficient distance to admit of inside box shutters. The latter to be of white pine inches thick, and fitted with best fastenings. Outside Venetian Blind shutters of the best workmanship, and fitted with best inside and outside fastenings, to be fitted to all the windows in all the stories except .

Casings.—All architraves or casings of the doors and windows in this and the second story to be made of the style, dimensions, and mouldings, as per plan and working drawings annexed. Solid *grounds* for all casings shall be fixed by the carpenter before any plastering is done, and no casings shall be put up till the walls are sufficiently firm to enable the joiner to make firm and close joints.

Bases in all the rooms in this story $1\frac{1}{2}$ inches thick, and inches high, moulded as per drawings, and grooved into the floor plank.

Piazza.—Build the piazza of the dimensions and style represented in plan. The columns to be of and the ceiling to be of ; and the floor of inch narrow yellow pine plank, tongued and grooved.

STAIRS.—Build the principal stairs with steps each rising inches, with treads inches broad. The steps to be 1½ inches thick, with moulded nosings, the risers 1½ inches thick: neat-moulded string 2½ inches thick. Newel, balusters, and handrail of mahogany, size and style as per drawings.

SECOND STORY.—FLOORS [here repeat foregoing details with the necessary alterations].

PARTITIONS.

WINDOWS.

SHUTTERS.

DOORS.

ATTIC.—FLOORS.

PARTITIONS.

WINDOWS.

SHUTTERS.

DOORS.

CLOSETS.—The pantry and closets, in dining, store-room, and kitchen, marked on the plans, to be thoroughly fitted up with all such shelves and closets as the proprietor may direct, as well as all closets in bed-rooms and passages; the latter also to be well provided with the necessary wardrobe hooks for clothes.

WATER-CLOSETS.—Fit up in a complete manner the water-closet, with all the necessary wood-work. The seat and rises to be of clear white pine [or mahogany], and all the work to be done as the plumber requires it, to make the whole perfect; including a strong cistern case, made of 2 inch pine, that will hold gallons of water: with a cover to the same.

The whole of the exterior wood work, and all not hitherto described, including carvings, mouldings, fixtures, cornices, and all other wooden architectural ornaments to make the building complete, according to the plans and elevations, to be made of clear, seasoned white pine, put together with white lead, and of the forms and sizes shown on the drawings; the whole to be done according to the directions, and to the satisfaction of the architect.

The carpenter and joiner are to find all the necessary materials, and all labor, tools, and every species of *hardware* and *ironmongery*, including all nails, bolts, bars, hinges, fastenings, and everything required for the completion of their work; and to prepare and fix all kinds of beads, stops, fillets, grounds, linings, and backings required for the perfect execution of the above, whether the same is herein specified or not; the whole to be executed in the most substantial and workmanlike manner, and to be done subject to the conditions hereto subjoined.

BELL-HANGER.

Provide and fix bells with best springs from the following places to . The wires of the same to be carried in tin tubes, fixed in the walls before the second coat of plaster is put on, and arranged in the best mode, with all necessary cranks, copper wire, &c. The bell pulls to be of and worth each.

PAINTER AND GLAZIER.

The GLAZIER shall glaze all the sashes in the basement story with crown glass: all the sashes in the principal story with the best crown (or plate) glass, selecting the best squares for the best apartments; and all the sashes in the second story and attic with best crown glass: all to be properly bedded, sprigged, and back-puttied, and left whole and clean on the completion of the building.

The PAINTER shall prime and paint the whole of the external wood work, iron work, and tin and copper work of the house, four coats of good English white lead in oil, the white lead being mixed with other colors, to bring it to the shade designated by the architect. The outer doors shall be painted .

The whole of the internal woodwork of the house (except floors and shelves) to be painted three coats in oil; the last coat in the principal floor, to be *flatted* (*i. e.*, turpentine used instead of oil, to take off the gloss). The doors and all wood work in shall be grained in the best style, in imitation of and, together with the handrails and balusters, &c., shall be varnished twice with the best copal varnish.

The painter shall knot, pumice down, and properly prepare all wood work before painting it; and the painter and glazier shall find all the materials, workmanship, and carriage, and everything necessary to the performance of their work, and to perform the same in a substantial and workmanlike manner, subject to the conditions of the contract.

PLUMBER AND TIN-SMITH.

The PLUMBER and TIN-SMITH shall provide and fix, as the progress of the work requires it, all necessary strips or flashings of inches wide, which shall be let into the brick work, where the roof joins the brick walls: also provide and fix aprons around all the chimney shafts let into the brick work, to throw the wet from the wall. Lay the gutters with inches broad. Where the same are against walls, turn up the strips

7 inches; where against rafter slopes, 10 inches. Cover the hips, ridges, and valleys of the roof with inches broad; the whole to be lapped, dressed, and nailed with lead-headed nails, and made perfectly tight. Provide and fix [tin, copper] leaders of inches in diameter from all the gutters on side of the house to the cistern, and from the side to the drain. Fit the cistern with inch supply and waste pipes. Line the sinks with lead weighing lbs. to the square foot, and provide and fix the necessary drainage pipe from the same.

Provide and fit up the water-closet in every respect perfect and complete, with soil pipe of 8 lb. lead, with D. trap, of 's manufacture and 4½ inch bore, to lead into drain, 1 inch supply pipe to the basin, and every other fixture and apparatus, to make the whole complete. Line the supply cistern pipe with 8lb. lead, and leave the whole in warranted working order.

Provide a bathing-tub of with waste pipe 1½ inches in diameter, leading into the drain, and fit up the same in the bathing room with all the necessary pipes, boilers, and shower-bath apparatus, complete. Fix all the pipes and water works from to and leave the whole in working order when the house is finished. Provide and fix a pump of the best quality.

The painter and glazier, plumber and tin-smith, and bell-hanger, shall also find all the materials, workmanship, and carriage, and whatever else shall be necessary to the performance of their works, and shall perform the same in a substantial and workmanlike manner; subject to the conditions of the contract.

CONDITIONS

For the performance of the several works in the respective trades, as set forth in, and according to the accompanying SPECIFICATIONS, *viz.*:

The contractor shall and will, at his own costs and charges, find, provide, and deliver, all and every kind of *new materials* of the best quality and description; together with the goods and chattels, cartage, scaffolding, tackle, tools, templets, rules, moulds, matters and things, labor and work, which may be necessary for the due, proper, and complete execution; and accordingly erect, build, execute, perform, finish, and complete, in a good, sound, and workmanlike manner (to the perfect satisfaction and approbation of the architect), the several buildings and works, agreeably and conformably, in all and every respect, to the specification, drawings, dimensions, and explanations, and observations thereon, or herein stated, described, or implied, and all things incident thereto, which may become necessary, according to the true intent and meaning thereof, although not specifically stated or described by (but which may be inferred from) the aforesaid drawings and specification, the same, generally, to illustrate each other. And, should it appear that any of the works hereby intended to be done, or matters relative thereto, are not fully detailed or explained in the said particular or drawings, the said builder or builders shall apply to the Architect for such further detailed explanations, and perform his orders as part of the contract.

The contractor, his foreman, or clerk, shall, upon or within forty-eight hours after receiving written notice from the architect, at any time and at all times, remove from the ground or buildings, whether worked or otherwise, all materials which may be unsound, improper, and not corresponding with the specification or drawings, and these conditions, and not approved by him; and substitute and bring back good and proper materials in lieu thereof; and in case of default therein, the architect shall be at liberty so to do, at the cost and charges of the contractor.

In case of delay by the contractor in providing and delivering the requisite materials, or in the advancement of the buildings, or works, or of a deficiency of workmen, as well in respect to dismissing any unskilful workman or workmen, or for misconduct, the architect shall be at liberty (after giving to, or leaving for, the contractor, his foreman, or clerk, six days' notice in writing) to provide, at the expense of the contractor, all such materials, and employ an increased number, or such number of workmen, at such wages as the architect shall think proper; and the costs and charges incurred, shall be retained out of the contract amount, or balance thereof, which may remain due, or be recoverable as liquidated damages. The architect to be at liberty to make any deviation from, or alteration in, the plan, form, construction, detail, and execution, described by the drawings and specification, without invalidating or rendering void the contract; and in case of any difference in the expense, an addition to, or abatement from the said contract amount shall be made, in the ratio or proportion such work may bear to the *whole* contract works, agreed to be performed, and the same to be determined by the architect; but no extra or addition to be admitted or allowed for, unless executed under written authority, and a statement and amount of claim be made weekly, for the architect's decision thereon.

The architect's opinion, certificate, report, and decision on all matters, to be binding and conclusive.

The contractor, his foreman, or clerk, upon receiving a written order from the architect for that purpose, shall suspend the working and proceeding with such part or portions of work, to be specified in such order, for the due and proper execution of *other* work or works connected therewith; and in case of frost or inclemency of weather, to effectually cover, protect, and secure the several works, as occasion may require, and prevent admission of wet through the apertures, and all damage occasioned thereby or otherwise, during the progress of the works, and by depredation or fire; the same to be borne and reinstated by, and at the expense of, the contractor, who is also to case effectually with boarding all bases, capitals, cornices, and other projections, and deliver up the building in the most perfect order and condition, fit for use and occupation.

The several works in erecting the building and finishing the same, to be proceeded in with all reasonable and proper despatch, in the several parts, consistently with the due and proper execution thereof (*here state the various works to be completed within given periods*).

And all the remaining carpenter's, joiner's, smith's, plasterer's, glazier's, painter's, and all other works, matters and things, in and about the building, as shown by the drawings, or stated in the specification, and herein, shall be completed on or before the day of under penalty of $ for every week exceeding those periods; and this condition not to be made or rendered void by any alteration or additional works being performed; but in such case the time shall be extended as shall be deemed proper by the architect and agreed to by the contractor, in writing, at the time of such extension.

The contractor will be required to find and provide two sureties for the due performance of his contract, to be bound each in the penal sum of $ and also to bear and pay the expense of the contract, which is to be prepared by the solicitor, to the employer.

Payments for the said works to be made by instalments, equal to per cent. on the amount of works, which shall be done and fixed.

The first payment when

The second payment when

The third [fourth, fifth or last] when the remaining works are completed; such payments to be made only when certified, in writing, by the architect, to have become due and payable; and within months after the whole works, matters and things, are completed and adjusted, and true balance stated and certified by the said architect; the contractor to receive the remaining part of the money due to him, and to give a receipt in full of all demands.

Provided, That the wages of artisans and laborers, and all those employed by the contractor, shall have been paid and satisfied, so that they shall have no lien upon the building or works.

It is hereby agreed,

This day of in the year , between of , on the one part, and on the other part, that he the said for himself, his executors, administrators, and assigns, doth hereby promise and agree, to and with the said to do and perform all the works, of every kind mentioned and contained in the foregoing particulars, and according and subject to the conditions above-recited, and according to the drawings prepared and referred to, at and for the sum of lawful money of the United States; and the said doth hereby agree to abide by and be subject to the several clauses, conditions, and penalties herein before-mentioned and contained.

In consideration whereof, the said doth hereby promise and agree to pay to the said on the certificate of the architect, the aforesaid sum of dollars, in separate payments, as before stated in the conditions.

In witness whereof, the said parties have hereunto set their hand, the day and year above written.

Witness,

HINTS TO YOUNG ARCHITECTS.

HINTS TO YOUNG ARCHITECTS.

PART I.

In a volume published some years ago by the late Mr. James Fraser, entitled "The Palace of Architecture," it was my aim to address at once the professional student and the general reader, by placing the subject of Architecture before them in a more popular and pictorial form than had theretofore been attempted. In respect to the *profession*, it presumed no further than to excite in the novitiate that feeling for the *romance* of his art which is not always elicited in the practice of an architect's office, and to promote in his mind a more catholic feeling for Architecture in its most comprehensive sense, than the confined circumstances of national and local requirement might be expected to encourage.

It is now my object to afford a sequel to that volume of a purely *practical* nature: to supply a course of hints which may prove serviceable, in the first instance, to the youth who is destined for the profession; and, in the second, to the young man who is about to enter upon the practice of it on his own account.

And, first, for the mere candidate who has yet to complete the last two years of his school studies. We presume that he has achieved a certain respectable quantum of classical attainment, with, at least, such a knowledge of the French language as it is now usual to afford in all well ordered schools. Still cultivating these, it now becomes essential that peculiar care be given to the promotion of practical mathematics, geometrical drawing, and perspective. By the former we mean all that relates to the formation and measurement of superficial and solid figures, and those parts of arithmetic which have reference to square and cubical estimate and valuation; plane trigonometry, essential to the operations of the surveyor; and mechanics, necessary to compute the strength and strain of materials. By geometrical drawing is meant the free use of the compasses and steel pen, the drawing board and T square, the camel-hair brush, and Indian ink: this to be followed by an industrious application to linear perspective.

Nothing is more common than for a young gentleman to enter an architect's office incapable of striking a circle without, at least, two ends; or of describing an octagon with any two sides alike; equally ignorant of cross multiplication—that leading essential of valuation practice, and bugbear of indolent reluctance; with no knowledge whatever of the use of the theodolite or spirit level; and having no idea that mechanics have any immediate reference to the permanent adaptation of stone and timber. A superficial reading of Euclid, and a course of algebra, may have gained a silver medal to be worn triumphantly on the last "breaking up day;" but the peculiar application of the study to such matters as especially concern the architect will not have been thought of; and a thousand facilities, which might have been readily afforded before the day of apprenticeship, have been omitted, to the great prejudice of subsequent pursuit. The self-flattering notion of manhood, natural to the emancipated youth, no longer a school-boy, is disgustingly corrected by the necessary incipient drudgery which makes him feel a child again—or leaves him the alternative of thinking himself too much a man for "task work" so elementary.

His knowledge of drawing is illustrated by a series of rather free copies of very picturesque originals, in which there is but little of the formality of vertical or horizontal lines, and still less of lines perspectively convergent. Significations of trees, cottages, cows, and ploughmen home returning, all beautifully mounted, with gold lines ruled around, are exhibited to his future master, as proofs of certain removes from nature without any approach towards art. If he have any artistical feeling for *landscape*, the chances are he will not be *architecturally* inclined. If architecturally given, it is not unlikely that his "drawing master" will have done his best to counteract the impulse. His geometrical drawing has been probably confined to a clumsy imitation of the figures of his Euclid, with letters that are *capital* only in a typographical sense. His writing :—ah, there indeed he flourishes! Words stretching out like race-horses, with long heads and tails raking into the lines above and below, so as to preserve a perplexing connexion between whole sentences, past, present, and to come!

Now, whatever may be necessary to other professions, or to any other branch of science or art, unquestionably there is no one which has more decidedly among its first principles the imperative law of PRECISION than that of an architect, whether it regards the operations of the mind or the hand. The responsibilities which attach to him, who may have to erect a large and important edifice, in which the economy of construction is to afford giant strength with graceful lightness, are such as should be considered from the very first moment of his architectural aspiration. *Precision*, then, in advancing, step by step, through all the gradations of initiatory study, demands the closest care. Architectural beauty is, in fact, the result of constructive perfection; and this can only be secured by laying down the first stone with a caution anticipating the pride that will attend the elevation of the crowning pinnacle. Each intermediate grade of operation will be also fulfilled with prospective and retrospective reference to all the others. The purpose and beauty of a building are indeed important; but the "very life of the building" is the foundation—*most* important, though afterwards to remain unseen. Many are the young architects who, on getting into practice, have had suddenly to make good with hasty, anxious, and health-destroying application, the omissions of their student years; and all, we maintain, from the early disregard of that precision of habit which, in the mind, means close and systematic study, and which indicates itself in the neatness and care of the hand.

But, while the young aspirant is not expected to have an intuitive sense of all this, neither is it to be supposed that he can, unaided, duly weigh its importance; and we therefore, through him, address those who have the care of his school studies after his profession may have been suggested. It will, at least, be unsafe, whether reasonable or not, to reckon upon any especial personal supervision at the hands of his professional master. His premium will be paid for the opportunities which he will have of learning—as his master learned before him; and in consideration of his ultimately securing to himself some of that remunerative practice which will be consequently forfeited by the senior professor. Moreover, it will assuredly be an all-sufficient answer for those, who expect personal instruction, to say that all existing practitioners of any note have depended on their own employment of the mere opportunity for self-tuition.

It is, therefore, in regard to the duty which the student owes to himself (for he may, to a sufficient extent, do his master's business, and yet neglect his own) that we emphasize the necessity of a certain amount of school training preparatory to the deed of apprenticeship. During the term of his articles, we presume not to meddle with him further than to call on him to do his best, as he may rest well assured the more he serves his master the more he will serve himself. After that, we shall venture to take him up again; for circumstances may prevent his gathering from his more competent adviser those *extra-official* instructions which it will be our hope to afford him.

To recur, then, to his closing school studies.

We begin with the most simple. The writing master is first

in request. The hand which usually wins the silver pen is about the worst that can be cultivated. We were ourselves nearly successful in the trial, and the mortification we experienced in having afterwards to curtail our capitals and control the comet-like eccentricities of our little *l*s and *p*s is not forgotten to this day. It was long before we could achieve the credit of being competent to write out the "fair copy" of a "specification;" and many were the plans we rendered slovenly by a want of neatness and clearness in our figurings. The desire to give an official-like character to a "detailed estimate" was frustrated during almost the whole of our apprenticeship; and as to "printing" the titles of the fair drawings with the relative designation of the PLANS, ELEVATIONS, and SECTIONS, there was a charity school office-boy who ever maintained in this particular an envied ascendency. Our good master used truly to say, that the writing and lettering would make respectable an indifferent drawing, and spoil a good one.*

The acquirement of a neat, close, and uniform character of writing, with practical ability in the several modes of lettering employed on drawings, is of immediate, and of no unimportant use in an architect's office. The student, thus prepared, comes into the instant participation of advantages which otherwise he must wait for. The perfecting of his penmanship may be fully acquired at school, and he might there also so practise it as to make it still more essentially serviceable by copying out, for instance, a compendious architectural glossary, and giving to each leading word the particular letter which typographically expresses it. Thus, terms having exclusive application to classical architecture might be in the ROMAN character; those exclusively confined to gothic architecture in the **OLD ENGLISH**; and all others of common meaning in *ITALICS:*

* We improved, however, marvellously, in our ordinary handwriting, and it was the mere penmanship of a letter of solicitation that a few years after obtained employment for us in the office of the late Sir John Soane.

the description being of course appended in the best kind of *Running Hand.* As a further exercise in the latter character, it would be well to copy out a dictionary of the technical terms of masonry, carpentry, &c.; the whole of which form no very lengthy operation, and would leave the practical illustrations of the office to be in their turn more interesting, because more readily comprehended.

The drawing master comes next. What may be now his practice in schools we know not; but, in our own time, he did but very little in the promotion of artistical truth, and nothing at all in the way of practical utility. If the intended architect have—as indeed he should have—a feeling for the *pictorial* of art, it will not ultimately suffer under the requirement of its more anatomical and geometrical necessities. A decision of hand in outline delineation is the very first desideratum in an architectural draughtsman. This applies not less to curved than to direct lines; nor can a better study be suggested than that of the human figure, beginning with the skeleton, combined with the representation of plain solids of regular form, without (in the first instance) any shading or attempt at *effect.*

When the hand has acquired some independent precision and firmness, the use of the mathematical instruments, drawing board, T square, and parallel ruler, should be carefully attended to; and all this will be sufficiently induced in the study of perspective. The pupil will first draw the plan of his subject, then the elevation, and finally work out its perspective appearance under certain prescribed conditions. His previously required precision of hand is now regulated by the knowledge of

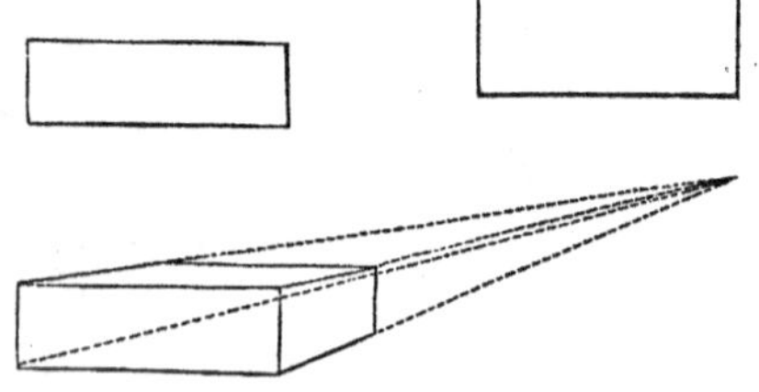

rule; and both will work together to make a correct and ready sketcher. The study of the finished human figure (which

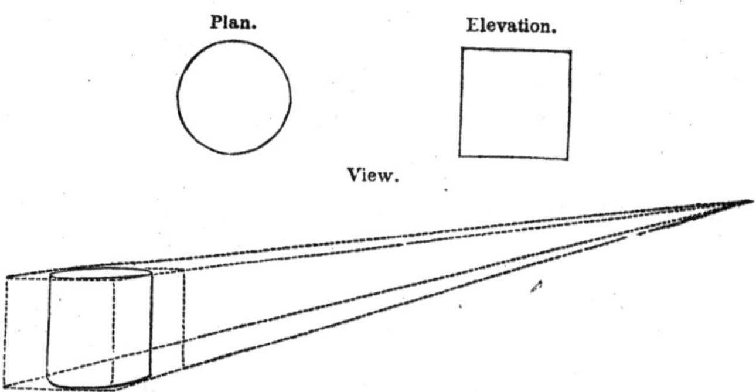

should alternate with the more formal process), while in itself most valuable in respect to statuesque architecture, will equally facilitate the drawing of mouldings and their enrichments ; and we may here add, that a careful copying of the leading frieze ornaments, Greek and Roman and Gothic, will be infinitely more to the purpose than any attempts at that mediocrity in picture which never afterwards aspires to more than a place in my lady's album.

A certain advance being thus made in linear drawings (which, by the way, having been first carefully pencilled, should then be more carefully perpetuated, with the steel or reed pen in Indian ink), the camel-hair brush will be introduced. To produce a smooth and uniform tint, accurately terminating with the boundary lines, is the first step ; to practise the "softening off" necessary to give effect to a circular pillar or a sphere, the next. The distinctions between positive and reflected light, shade and shadow, will succeed ; and then will follow the leading rules by which shadows are accurately projected. After this, it will be time to indulge in the charms of color ; and, when the student has mastered the means of dealing with superficies and solids, his drawing master may then do his best to make an artist of him.

The late Mr. Peter Nicholson has done all that is necessary to enable the school tutors to direct their pupils both in the preparatory movements of architectural drawing, and in the leading application of mechanics to architectural practice; and this brings us to speak of the latter.

As a mere act of mental discipline, a course of the classics will be of equal value with mechanics; but the practical value of the latter will be at once apparent when it is considered, that the means of constructing every building involve the use of all the mechanical powers, and that a knowledge of the properties of the simplest of these—the lever—is of the utmost importance as affecting the laws of the resistance of timber, the composition and resolution of forces. The construction of roofs, overhanging partition framings, and trussed beams, becomes a matter of prominent interest, when the mechanical principles on which it depends are understood; and all we contemplate, in speaking of the young architect in embryo, is the guidance of his mind into that train of practical thought which the obvious *utility* of his early studies will promote. There is nothing to prevent a school-boy from mastering such brief elementary articles as those of Mr. Gwilt on "the Equilibrium of Arches" and the necessary magnitude of their piers; or such as Mr. Bartholomew's Chapters on Gravity, "the source of all principle and defect in architectural construction;" nor can we resist an allusion to the Articles on Masonry and Carpentry, published in a separate form, from the Encyclopædia Britannica.

Allusion has been made to the arithmetical and mathematical studies of the intended architect. It is most due to the value of his time when he first enters the office of his professional master, that he should be already fully practised in all that relates to square and cube measure; quick and sure in the working of cross multiplication, and in carrying out the sums, or what is termed the "moneying" of quantities at different prices. It will not be his business, until he is apprenticed, to learn the different ways in which the differing branches of artificers' work are measured; or their value *per* yard, *per* foot, *per* rod, or *per* perch, superficial or cube; but he ought to have at his finger ends the mere calculative process, so that his attention may be given, from the first day of his entering an office, to acquiring a knowledge of the nature and value of labor and materials, and of the varied way in which the mason, bricklayer, plasterer, carpenter and joiner, plumber and painter, compute their perfected operations. All the ordinary rules of arithmetic are of course of absolute necessity. We only speak of those in reference to which the *utmost practical readiness* is immediately required. He who can square the greatest number of dimensions in the least possible time; in like manner multiply quantities by prices, and "add up" a foot long of closely written pounds, shillings, and pence, has received, as it were, an impetus which will carry him upwards on the ascent of early practice, and vastly alleviate the tedium of this most imperative drudgery.

His mathematical studies should in the same degree facilitate the construction, with his compasses and steel pen, of circles, squares, triangles, pentagons, octagons, and so on to polygons, divided and sub-divided,—of parallels that have no chance of meeting, and truncated isosceles triangles that have their apex in some unattainable point beyond the other end of the school-room. Trigonometrical practice, too, might be carried on at least so far as to produce a map of the play-ground, including "the duck-pond and three elm trees beyond," with the respective levels of the several angle points. He should be enabled to raise a perpendicular line without his drawing board and T square, and to draw a raking line at any required angle. Of the many things which are generally only touched upon at schools, such leading ones as we have mentioned should be fairly grasped. A three years' term would be thereby rendered equal to the usual five; and, at the end of the five, a salary might be commanded, where a mere interval of anxious incompetency is the common instigation to forfeit *more* time, in making good the loss of time past.

We have spoken of some knowledge of French as usually afforded at schools. The more of it that can be there attained, without injury to the immediate essentials before enumerated, the better; because, in conjunction with Latin, it promotes those facilities of travel, of which we sincerely hope our intended young architect may be enabled to avail himself. At all events then, what *can* be learned at school should not afterwards be forgotten; and this prompts us to make the only reference in which we shall indulge as to the duty of the student during his apprenticeship. After Latin and French, *Italian* is easily acquired. The study of this simple and beautiful language (speaking of it as a medium of communication, and plain literary instruction) will prove a mere pastime. The writer of these hints (though naturally slow at languages) learned sufficiently, by two months' *exclusive* application, to read simple prose readily, and to make his way through Italy tolerably well.

During the term of his articles, we would therefore recommend him to give uninterrupted, though easy attention, to French and Italian, making the latter perhaps the more especial as he proceeds. There are numerous works in both languages in which architecture, both as a *science* and *art*, is most ably treated on; and we are free to confess our envy of that knowledge of German which enabled Mr. W. H. Leeds to afford to his countrymen a translation of Moller's "Memorials of German Gothic Architecture."

Lastly, we would impress upon the young aspirant to architectural honors, our repetition of the RESPONSIBILITIES which will attach to him from the first hour of his unaided practice. It may be some time before he will be enabled to purchase assistance; and, during that state of individual probation, he will have—if he have employment—duties relatively more arduous and more harassing, than when commissions shall thereafter pour upon him to the hoped-for advancement of his fame and fortune. He must be for a time "grand master," assistant surveyor, and drudgery clerk, of his own establishment: at once designer artistical, constructor practical, copying draughtsman, measurer, valuer, and more—with which we would not frighten him. He must cultivate resolution on the ground of knowledge, endurance on that of patience, and modesty on the full assurance, that, when he shall have practised to the last day of his occupation, he will have learned the more to know how much he has yet to learn. His profession is a noble one, based on palpable science, and beautified by the poetry of art. It is most gratifying in respect to the society to which it may lead, and the rank it may confer. It is more especially so in regard to the pride which an architect cannot but feel in contemplating the material and enduring majesty of the structures he may have to raise. Paintings must be sought in the gallery; statues may indeed preside in the open square; but it is architecture only which towers into the sky—alike commanding, far or near; and combining the graces of form, proportion, and decoration, with picturesque charm and massive grandeur.

We now take leave of our school student, to meet him again some five years hence.

PART II.

Our quondam school-boy is now, in reality, a "young architect." He has "served his time" in the office of some established professor and practitioner, and we have only to hope that his time has served him. Presuming that it *has* done so, even to a greater degree than is usual, he must still consider, not only that he has much to learn,—but something to *un*-learn,—for the *mannerisms* of his master have, most likely, a present influence upon him to the prevention of the due development of his native taste and feeling. He must consider that he has been hitherto exercised only in those particular styles of the art which his tutor has been called upon to practise, and that he (the pupil) may have, in his future career, to deal with other styles, and even with the same styles in a novel manner. He may have, not only new combinations to effect, but also original, or hitherto unrevived, features to study. He has to get the wheels of his mind out of the ruts of habitual office practice, and to drive the coursers of his imagination over the free common ground of varied and speculative design. He has, no doubt, acquired much *artistical* knowledge that is true, and much *practical* attainment that is valuable; but the very conditions of his pupilage have enforced an obedience, which, though most wholesome in respect to discipline, has yet trammelled his invention and checked his fancy. Young architects will be generally found to criticise the works of others by the standard of their master's; and, by the way, they are usually much given to criticism, with a greater aptitude for censure than eulogy—the natural result of limited knowledge bearing upon comprehensive variety.

Now, to get rid of the mere bonds of habit, there is, unquestionably, nothing so certainly efficacious as TRAVEL.

> " Home-keeping youth have ever homely wits.
> I rather would entreat thy company
> To see the wonders of the world abroad ;
> For it may be impeachment to thy age
> In having known no travel in thy youth.
> Experience is by industry achieved,
> And perfected by the swift course of time ;
> Nor can he hope to be a perfect man,
> Not being tried nor tutor'd in the world."

Submissive obedience has been already sufficiently practised. A lively and acute observation has now to be cultivated. What is sterling in the range of former acquirement will not be lost nor diminished. The ever fresh air of changing scenes and differing countries,

> " Puffing at all, winnows the light away,
> And what hath mass, or matter, by itself
> Lies rich in virtue, and unmingled."

Corrective in respect to *past* studies, travel will prove also highly suggestive in regard to the studies which are to follow ; and the young artist, instead of remaining a critic over others, will find enough to do in criticising himself.

Nor let it be supposed that the benefits of travel are less than they formerly were, because books have multiplied to us the labors of former travellers. The object of travel, it is true, is not so elementary as it was, ere Stuart and Revett, Denon, Taylor, Cressy, and others, had afforded all necessary information as to the details of Greek, Egyptian, and Roman design ; but it is, as ever, important in expanding the taste for the beautiful and picturesque, and in stimulating that professional enthusiasm which can only be excited by beholding the actual realities whose distant features we have previously learned to appreciate.

Apart from the more professional and technical matters of a young architect's travel, are others of a moral and social kind not less to be considered. It has been said that "manners make the man," and in no case is the saying worthier than in that of an architect, who depends not more on his ability to answer the duties of employment than on the address and conduct necessary to form and secure a connexion. Of all men engaged in the polite art, he is the most frequently and continuously in personal communication with his patron. The sources of conversation which travel affords, and the polish which it may be reasonably expected to occasion, are obviously of no mean value to one, who may be constantly the table guest and resident visitor of his employer. An accomplished architect is necessarily a man competent, to talk at least, if not to evince in some measure a practical attainment of Art in general. A feeling for elegant literature is also a natural concomitant of the critical refinement which his reading should have secured to him. The knowledge of the continental languages will not have been acquired without some acquaintance with the leading authors who have employed them; and an experience of continental society will not have been effected without an improvement in his behavior. Many are the instances of young men having formed those intimacies among their own countrymen abroad which have subsequently proved most productive at home; and certain it is, that he who has enriched his portfolio with evidences of his industry in Rome, Florence, and Venice, will find an advantage in its mere possession as a credential, though otherwise it may serve him but little.

The truth is, there is no longer any occasion for him to risk his neck in clambering the arcades of the Coliseum, or to spend his time in measuring the portico of the Pantheon. So far, at least, as it regards the details of Egyptian, Greek, Roman Gothic, Moorish, and Byzantine architecture, his work is already done for him. If he cannot possess himself of the books themselves, he may have ready access to libraries, in which every important feature of these varieties of design is elaborately and truthfully delineated. It is his sketch and note book, rather than his measuring rod, which should occupy his foremost attention. He requires less to fill his paper with dimensions than his mind with IDEAS. He now wants feelings rather than facts; correctives rather than corroborations; motives rather than materials; speculative freedom rather than academical precision. This is the time for him to cultivate the poetry of his art, ever attentive to those high and catholic principles of design, which, though the same in essence, develope themselves in different forms suitable to the climate, the manners, the religious or social state of the different countries through which he successively passes. He will by no means confine himself, as was the case formerly, to *antiquity*. He will take observant cognisance of the numerous illustrations of medieval modification; and still more of all examples of more modern excellence. In two instances only will he remain exclusive in his devotion; viz., to *ancient sculpture* and the *old masters of historical art*. Let him remember, that Architecture raises the temple which Painting and Sculpture are to occupy as their own loved home; and that, as he may have to co-operate with the painter and sculptor in the production of "one entire and perfect" work, it is a duty he owes to his fellow laborers to cultivate an adequate feeling for their respective portions of it. He alone, who is in some degree a painter and sculptor (*i. e.* critically), can be competent to the honor of their copartnership. If the young architect be inclined to carry it further than criticism, the period of his travel is the time for his operations. Then may he well varv his pursuits with drawings from the antique, and with sketches from the grand frescoes of Raphael and Buonarotti ; but especially with exercises in water color from Italy's own Nature, in her combinations with architectural forms. Highly advantageous is it for every architect to become a correct and ready sketcher, a master of eye-perspective, and a creditable performer with his brush and colors. The fascinations of smart and lightly managed effects of sun, shadow, and tint, will some day "tell" in his favor ; and he may now be engaged in preparing for his future drawing-room pictorial decorations, which shall also be of important service to him as so many official insignia, "flags and signs" of the love he bears to the profession he has adopted.

His more practical drawing will be well applied to choice selections from the architectural fragments which may excite his admiration in the several great Italian Museums, all of which are prodigal in the exhibition of decorative art. The experience already acquired at home will teach him where such things may be hereafter suitable for application ; and his employer will not be the less pleased in learning, that the vase on his balustrade or the frieze on his chimneypiece are fac-similes of some valued importation from the "Museo Vaticano."

Italian Gothic he will carefully eschew—at least as a model. To the great Cathedrals of Germany, France, and Normandy, his *continental* Gothic studies will be confined; nor will he forget, even in perusing them, that England is, after all, more especially the school in which Gothic architecture developes itself with the most essential truth. In Normandy, the Norman Gothic is unquestionably better and more fully illustrated than with us ; and in many of the foreign pointed examples he will see certain individual parts of a far greater magnitude and more elaborate richness than any he can meet with at home ; but it is still from an untiring study of the cathedrals, churches, and old mansions of England, that the true principles of Gothic design, the laws of its proportion, and the most effective results of its combinations, are to be deduced.

The growing feeling in our country for the palatial style of medieval Rome and of Venice, and for the villa of modern Italy, will, of course, direct him to give more than common attention to such examples as best exhibit them; so that he may co-operate with his numerous improving contemporaries in working out a worthy Anglo-Italian school of design. Scientific and literary professors, travellers, high church conservatives, and others, have all built their club-houses in pursuance of the aim started by the Buonarottis and Palladios. Country gentlemen are raising their mansions in emulation of the landscape lords of Italy, with Corinthian porticos, balustraded terraces, and Belvedere towers. The Palladian palace of Stowe, and the grand piles of Blenheim and Castle Howard, still maintain their ascendency over all modern attempts at the castellated or Tudor mansion; and, while the Church Architectural Societies are effecting much good in the restoration of a pure and correct taste for Christian Pointed Architecture as applied to churches and other buildings ecclesiastically connected, there can be little doubt of the propagation and continued durability of a reviving love for the modifications of Greek and Roman design.

As to the time which should be occupied in travel, two years should be the utmost; while one, employed with devotional industry, may be sufficient. At all events, a longer period than the former may too much interfere with the business habits of a young architect who only has his profession to depend upon. The more limited period will allow of a month at Paris, two at Florence, four in Rome, one at Naples, one at Venice, and the remaining three for a general survey of the intervening cities and those on his northern route homewards. If, however, circumstances will allow it, the longer period may be well expended, and the moral and social advantages will of course be the better cultivated. The writer of these Hints was limited in time—because limited in means. Impressed with the fear of debt, and anxious to relieve those by whose kind aid he was advantaged, his "travel's history" scarcely filled the twelvemonth. The cost of his travelling, lodging, and other incidentals, did not exceed ninety-two pounds, about twenty more having been expended in books and other articles of professional utility. To him the pleasures of society (save those he enjoyed at the common mess-table of his brother artists) were denied. Excursions of relaxation and mere enjoyment were out of the question. He witnessed one opera at Milan, because it was his duty to inspect the grand Scala theatre; and made pleasure and profit tell together in seeing at once the interior of a French theatre, and the acting of Talma. But he feared the expense of venturing south of Rome; forfeited the desired gratification of seeing Vesuvius and the disentombed cities of its vicinity, the gay beauties of Naples, and the solitary grandeur of Pæstum; and, after all, returned home with as much preserved cash as would have enabled him to accomplish what he had not dared to attempt. This was doubtless bad management, and will excite rather the smile of contempt than the sigh of sympathy. Prospects, however, are more cheering now. The then "poor student" is now a gratefully thriving architect; and, D. V., he will eat macaroni at Naples, *yet*.

PART III

Our traveller has now returned. His brass plate is upon his door. He has indentures to prove his apprenticeship, a portfolio to assert his subsequently acquired accomplishment ; and he is—ready to begin.

The probability is, that he'll have to wait awhile. He will have nothing to do—or what he does will be done for nothing. Some one will kindly give him an opportunity of showing what he *can* do : the favor shown, and the labor given, being mutually gratuitous. Advertisements will invite him to compete for a Town Hall, or a "New Bridewell," a Market House, or a New Poor Union : and he will send his plans forward ; and they will be sent back ; and some one, already well to do in his profession, will, as he is informed, either by favor, or job, or otherwise, win the premium and be commissioned to carry on the work : and thus will the rejected among many sit down disconsolate, and quote from Jaques—

> "Thou mak'st thy testament as worldlings do,
> Giving thy sum of more to that which had too much."

And then will he be stimulated by a promise from some worthy friend of his father, who expresses vague ideas of "some day adding a new dining-room to his house," under the inspiration of which, visions of a side-board recess, flanked by Corinthian columns, suggest themselves ; and, lastly, he who has promised nothing, shows his friendly indignation in abusing him whose promise has turned out to be nothing worth.

Hopes, disappointments, and efforts (for the present) unavailing, will (unless he be wondrously fortunate in chance or connexion) mark his career for some time at least ; *mais le bon temps viendra*, and we propose filling up the leisure of the interval by putting before him such matters for consideration, as may make him rather value, than otherwise, the spare time which yet lies upon his hands.

The duty he now owes to himself is two-fold. In the first place, he has to form and increase his connexion by constantly availing himself of every opportunity for manifesting his professional claims to desert. In the second place, he has to prepare himself for an effective and perfect fulfilment of the duties which his first engagement will impose upon him. We have already sought to impress upon him the heavy responsibility which will be his when he is no longer the mere agent of a professional superior. Let him not postpone this reflection until the day of employment arrive. Everybody is always in a hurry to have everything done. His patron will take six months to think of what he desires to have accomplished in as many hours. When the commission arrives, immediate work will be required—not preparatory study : and if there be not a ready foresight to pierce through all contingencies, the progressive and ultimate perplexity will be proportionally bewildering. To anticipate possible objections is greater policy in an architect than to give immediate answer to requirement. Of all professions, his is the one most subjecting its professor to meddling interference, and a thoughtless disregard of trouble taken and obedience unrequited.

> " Double, double,
> Toil and trouble,"

is indeed the chant of the sister Fates who are hostile to an architect's peace. The graces of the portico, the beauties of decoration and proportion, the triumph over a hundred contending desiderata, shall be all forgotten in my lady's passion for—a housemaid's closet ! It availeth not as an excuse that you can put it under the back stairs. " It should have been thought upon before. An architect ! and not think of a housemaid's closet ! It ought *not* to be an extra." " Extra !" Fearful word ! The builder's aim, and the architect's dread ! Let our young friend think of it betimes ; and let him bear in mind, that the best guard against the overwhelming censure which follows it, is to habituate the mind to a foresight, which, during a study of the nearest and most important things, should penetrate into the most remote and trifling. All the grand principles of design, convenience, and enduring strength, may have been perfectly answered by the most artistical ability, by ingenious arrangement, and constructive skill ; but, if chimneys smoke, gutters leak, or drains choke ; if windows prove not in all trials weather-tight ; if all the little conveniences of the former house be not added to all the larger ones of the present ; if a shelf, a cupboard, or a rail and pins be omitted where custom might expect to find them ; if the whims of old servants be not considered, or the carelessness of new ones anticipated ; if, in short, the genius of a Michael Angelo be not followed close up with the care of a cabinet-maker, the architect will yet have a toil of vexation to encounter which may make him almost repent the choice of his profession.

We shall begin our practical Hints with some remarks in reference to plans, or internal arrangement, as affecting elevations, roofs, and chimneys.

The young architect too frequently concentrates his attention on those portions of his plan which concern one or more particular façades. Thus, he is careful of his entrance front, and his lawn elevation, as those alone which will be visible to a stranger approaching from the lodge, or walking in front of the sitting-room windows ; and no sooner is the building roofed in than he discovers that the " return fronts" are provokingly more generally visib.e to the public eye from without the boundary of the premises than the others which have had his too exclusive care. One of his "architectural" elevations is seen in continuous connexion with a surface of unstudied masonry, the respective parts of which neither harmonize in position nor in decoration: or, at the best, he exhibits a display of blank architecture, the falseness of which is proved by certain prominent necessities which will not be either concealed or modified. The offices and other inferior appendages to the mansion cling to it, and proclaim themselves with all the humiliating impertinence (or rather *per*tinence) of poor relations bent on the declaration of their consanguinity. The idea of "planting them out," which originally existed in the mind of the designer, still exists in *his* mind only. The trees he requires will take at least fifty years to grow; and, even then, winter will in its turn disrobe them of their foliage to leave displayed an obstinate range of architectural poverty. Evergreens will *never* grow high enough. The whole thing must remain as it is—a handsome countenance with an ugly profile—a beggar in a velvet waistcoat, and no coat to cover his sides.

This oversight is still more commonly committed in town houses and street architecture. Nothing is more frequent among builders and young architects than the exhibition of a mere mask, which only deceives while the spectator is directly opposite on the other side of the street, or so far as there may be houses of equal height continuing on either hand. Otherwise, directly the front is passed, the blank masonry or naked gables of the returns show themselves like the mere party-walls in the transverse section of an unfinished range; and these, be it remembered, are often seen for a much greater length of time than is given, in passing, to the main front, since we may have them before us during the whole of our progress along a street of half a mile extent. Perhaps only a portion of the return ends may be seen above the roofs of the lower houses adjoining: but it is not the less necessary to continue along this portion the architectural character of the front. In the many instances which occur of houses rising successively one above the other on the side of an ascending street, too much care cannot be taken to give a finished perspective effect. The means will readily suggest themselves to any one who is competent to take professional rank; and to such only do we now address ourselves. Architecture, as we have before said in the first Section of our Hints, has a peculiar privilege among the arts in commanding observation from the distance, and no town or range of buildings will ever have an imposing, or even a tidy appearance, while it shows itself to be composed of independent fragments jostling one against another. The beggarly habit of carrying a cornice or parapet, with dressed doors, windows, pilasters, &c., along a twenty-feet front, leaving in barn-like nakedness a thirty or forty-feet end, is an abomination which even the most vulgar country builder should eschew. Infinitely better that the whole should be consistent in the absolute perfection of nudity.

Oversights, however, sufficiently unpardonable are often exhibited by architects of more established repute, in settling their *plans* without due regard to the final appearance of their exteriors. We have now our mind's eye on a villa of severe Greek architecture, the internal disposition of which is as good as need be. The doors, windows, and fire-places, are properly disposed in reference to the rooms separately considered ; but the roof shows the most painful irregularities of form and height. In one place it ascends to cover a lofty ball-room, in another it descends below the parapet, and in another part are seen the glazing and leaded flat of a lantern-light. The chimneys start up indiscriminately from several parts of the roof in differing form, bulk, and elevation, and some of the flues are carried up in the thickness of the outer walls, having their outlets in tne parapet, where no rising stacks were, critically, admissible. The natural consequence was smoking rooms, and the remedy has been chimney-pots, ranged (as if to be pelted at) on the top of the parapet ! Now, in this instance, the patron was equally pleased with the Plans and the Elevations ; and it was not for *him* to see that they were incompatible. The culpability lay entirely with his architect, who either shamefully omitted in his drawings the disfigurements alluded to, or failed to consider, that, in the execution of his work, they would be inevitable. Let it, then, be the first care of the young architect in designing his *plan,* to do it with especial reference to the *style* of architecture which he is desired to adopt. In strictness, the style should be suggested by the internal arrangement ; but, either way, it is equally an architect's duty to see, that convenience and external expression be true to one another. A ground plan may be exactly adapted (by certain equally convenient differences of arrangement) either to a Greek or Roman, a Gothic or Italian Elevation ; and whichsoever of these may be decided on, the arrangements of the walls, with their breaks, recesses, and projections, and the position of the fire-places, must be thought of in close conjunction with the ranges and intersections of the roof, and the satisfactory position of the chimneys, as objects in the general view of the building. It is not, in fact, until a plan of the roof is made, with its stacks of flues well located and accurately drawn, that the masonry of the floors beneath can be decided on : nor should the plan of any one floor be *finished* until those of the floor or floors above are perfected.

These points being all considered, the young architect will take care to make his elevations honestly exhibit their crowning roof and chimneys. The custom of omitting these features is seriously reprehensible, and worthy only of a Pecksniff. He will be equally careful also, to show *all* the fronts, and to give at least such *perspective sketches* as may prevent those common misconceptions which *geometrical elevations* occasion in not truly showing the projecting or receding of the different portions. Even architects deceive themselves by the pleasing effect of façades geometrically developed ; an effect which is rarely seen in reality, except at such a distance as renders indistinct all the decorative details of the building. What a

false idea, for instance, does the geometrical figure A give of the perspective figure B ! It is not enough to show, by the plans or by description, that *c* projects and that *d d* recede. The strict truth is, that, in the perspective view most generally visible, the building will lose all the expression of *length* which pleases in the geometrical elevation, and will become a *short* squat building, with only one visible wing instead of two. The geometrical elevation of a circular temple is most deceptive in its appearance, and will occasion expectations of much greater width than a near perspective view will exhibit : thus, the building which will show geometrically as fig. 1, will show perspectively as fig. 2. In the elevation of the west front of

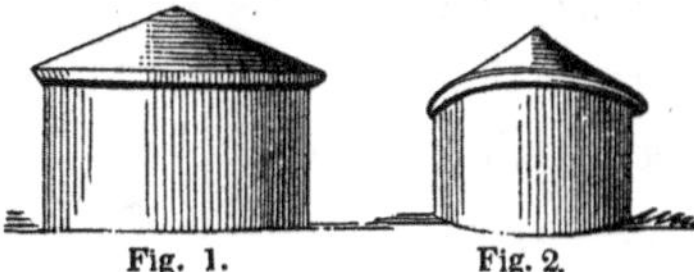

Fig. 1. Fig. 2.

St. Paul's Cathedral, the tambour of the dome looks overwhelmingly large ; in the view of the real building from a moderate distance it exhibits no such excess. Again, the geometrical elevation of a square tower, in which the expression of great altitude is required, should be made with reference to the increased bulk it will exhibit, when viewed diagonally, to the prejudice of its loftiness. The habit, in short, of considering the elevations of parallel planes, without equal regard to their "returns," and without studying the diagonal view of both united, is the cause of infinite disappointment ; and, equally so, is that of only looking point blank against edges and *vertical* surfaces, without duly reflecting on the additional effect of under, or upper, *horizontal* surfaces. For example; what a light and simple effect has the common cantilever cornice, fig. A, compared to the same cornice seen in perspective, as fig B. Features, which in the geometrical drawing may appear light and well-proportioned, may in execution prove ill-proportioned and heavy. Again, what may seem well developed in the drawing, may wholly or partially disappear in the work itself, as in the case of a parapet or blocking course concealed from the near view by the projection of the cornice. A dome which, geometrically, has a sufficient height, may, from the point of most frequent view, seem offensively flat. Sir C. Wren, aware of this, has formed the outline of St. Paul's dome by segments of circles struck from two centres like a Gothic arch, the point of meeting being concealed by the base of the lantern. Its *appearance*, however, is that of a perfect semisphere. There is also another precaution to be always carefully taken in the management of circular buildings, and this refers to the unpleasant effect of overhanging segmental architraves or soffits. A is the elevation of a window in a bow projection. B is its perspective appearance from one side. This is not less objectionable in respect to its constructive weakness than in regard to its ugliness; for it is only by concealed management that a soffit flat arch on a curved plan can be made to stand at all. The case is still worse when the window head is a curve, and, in short, this practice is only allowable when the curve of the plan is so large, and the openings so

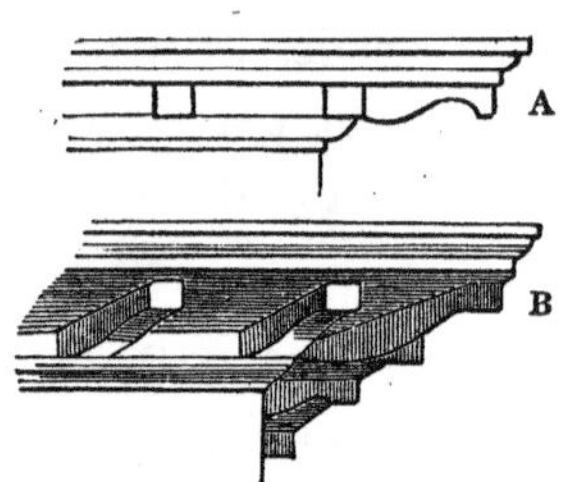

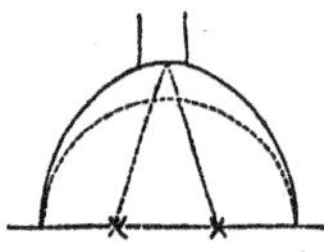

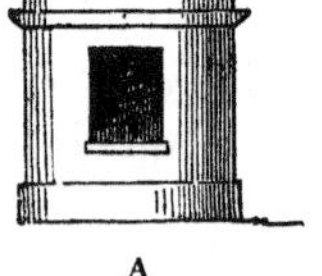

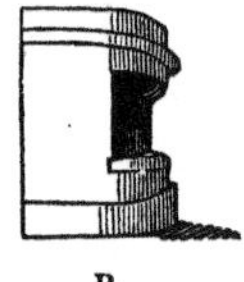

narrow, as not to leave perceptible the defect of the overhanging segment. Thus, in the vast curved outline of the Coliseum the arched colonnade is unobjectionable. In the closely-set peristyles of St. Paul's dome, and of the Temples of Vesta at Rome and Tivoli, it is equally so; but, where the curve of the plan is small, and the openings or spaces between the columns proportionally large, it is a grievous fault, which not even the wish of patronage should be allowed to sanction. Where small bay projections are desired, they should always be semi-hexagons or semi-octagons, with the windows in the flat faces, unless indeed the required bow window may be so subdivided by mullions or pilasters as to remedy the objections stated. The semicircular portico, fig. 1, may be sufficiently pleasing in its front view; but a glance at fig. 2 will show the necessity of studying, not fronts only, but profiles also.

Fig. 1.

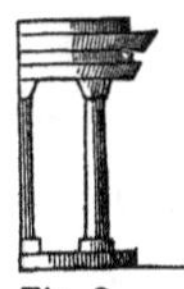
Fig. 2.

While on the subject of the different appearance of objects in different points of view, it may be as well to refer to the triangle as a form of plan frequently, and most injudiciously, adopted in pyramids, obelisks, and pedestals. Viewed directly in front, on the lines *a—b* or *c—d*, it is well enough, as shown by figs. 1 and 2; but who, that sees its appearance on the line *e—a*, as shown by fig. 3, does not at once observe that no pyramid or obelisk should ever have an odd number of sides? For the same reason, tripod pedestals should be most cautiously used; for, whatever may be said in favor of fig. 4, it is obvious nothing can be adduced in defence of so ill-balanced a composition as fig. 5.

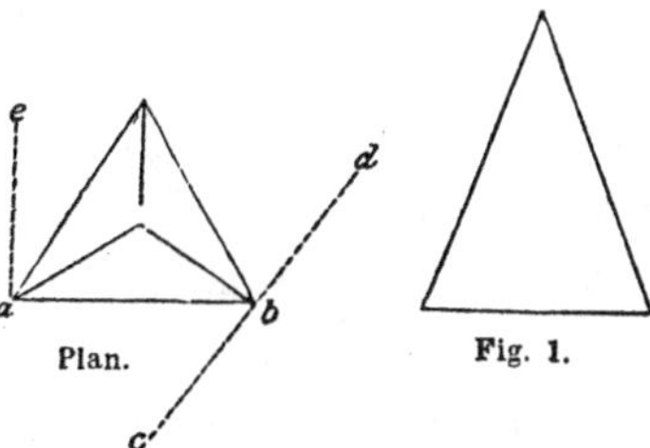

Plan. Fig. 1.

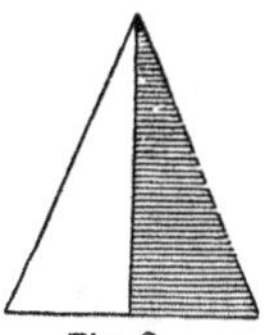
Fig. 2.

Fig. 3.

All this goes to prove the necessity—if not absolutely of models—of the perspective effects which buildings will have from all points of view. The architect, pleased with his front elevation, may find reason to alter it the moment he turns the corner. A different proportion in the solids and voids of a main and return elevation will be fatal to good effect. A material difference in the distances between the common angle and the windows of the front and return façades, or a much more crowded position of windows in the one than the other, will be offensive: and it may be here remarked, that the proportions of solid and void which hold good in the case of a simple façade with no dressings to its doors and windows, will not equally serve when those dressings are to be supplied, since it is only the *plain* part of the pier, or of the space between the lower and upper apertures, which will "tell" in the matter of *breadth*. The architraves and flanking columns of a window must be regarded as the window itself; and, as a general rule, it may be said, that there cannot be an adequate expression of breadth, unless the plain part of the pier be equal to the entire width of the window and its dressings united. The same law holds good in the horizontal spaces, which should exhibit, in a large and ornate building, the same amount of plain masonry above and below the architraves, strings, cornices, &c., which, in a small and plain building, would intervene between the sills and soffits of the windows and the strings or cornice below or above them. This, it may be remarked, amounts to little less than saying that architectural decoration is more applicable to large than small buildings; and it is true; for doors and windows do not increase in the same ratio that the size of the building increases. On the contrary, they generally bear a

Fig. 4. Fig. 5.

much greater relative proportion in poor men's houses than in princes' palaces; and, assuredly, where they do not leave, *at the very least*, such a breadth of pier as will allow the width of the opening to intervene between the dressings of two adjacent windows, the latter had better be left without dressings. On no occasion whatever ought the breadth of a pier to be ess than the width of a window opening; *i. e.* of course supposing the window to be a single one, and not triple with intervening *mullions*.

If the error of making a discordant difference between the fronts of the main house be so serious, not less so is the total discordancy often seen between the Main House and the Offices. Now, it is, in fact, very rarely that the offices are not, from several important points of view, seen in conjunction with the principal mass of the structure; and the difference, therefore, between the two should strictly be one of degree only. A handsome cornice along the eaves of the one will be ill-accompanied by a common shute along those of the other. Correctly speaking, it should be of the same form, reduced proportionally in scale, and—if required—without the enrichments of the main cornice. Above all things, the young architect should avoid the common mistake of reducing the beauty of the chimneys; for those of an office range, springing usually from a lower roof and having a greater relative altitude, will very likely be more conspicuous than the others. In short, an aptitude for chimney design is most important to an architect engaged in villa building. Let not the anticipation of chimney-pots escape his consideration. On the contrary, let him design them, and show them in his elevations, as likelihoods, which, if ultimately necessary, may not be absolutely disfiguring. He will further remember, that, where the flues in any one stack are numerous, it may be better to place them in united parallels than in one continuous range; and he will be also cautious in so arranging his fire-places as that the various flue-stacks may be as nearly as possible of one size. This uniformity, at all events, should be observed in corresponding pairs of stacks.

He need not be reminded, that, in Gothic structures, chimneys are not only admissible, but are often advantageous in their attachment to outer walls,—especially when they rise with the gables. In the free and irregular style of the Italian villa they may also occasionally be connected with the outer walls. In the severer Roman style they may rise from the angles (as shown in Barry's Reform Club-House); but in no style (saving only the Gothic) should they rise from the eaves if it can possibly be avoided. The inordinate height required to raise them above the ridge of the roof, their insecurity (involving often the application of iron struts to sustain them), the difficulty of a satisfactory management of the main cornice beneath them, and the plumbing required to make water-tight their union with the slates;—all these circumstances make it most desirable the plans should be so arranged, that the chimneys may ride, as it were, upon the ridges of the roof. The occasional practice of making flues run a long raking course in the thickness of walls, and of making them even turn corners to conduct them to a desirable position of exit, cannot be too seriously reprehended. Under-ground flues, too, which must be periodically opened to be cleaned, should never be adopted save under those imperative circumstances which the most industrious ingenuity cannot avoid. Never allow two flues to unite in becoming one; and above all things, so arrange the floor and roof timbers, that there shall be no chance of their being carried (even by carelessness itself) into the flues, or within at least nine inches of them. Here let us remark, while the occasion so seriously calls for it, on the necessity of an architect never trusting to the *sagacity* of workmen—especially in the country. The common carpenter and rubble mason will each do *his* work irrespective of the other's; and on visiting your building, you will very likely find that a joist or a purlin has little to divide it from the fury of a chimney on fire, except the plaster pargetting which lines the inside of the flue! With equal care, look to the work which receives the hearths of the fire-places. "Brick trimmer arches" may have been inserted in the specification; but, if there be not a clerk of the works to look after the building, it is by no means certain they will be constructed.

To recur to the subject of the offices and inferior buildings attached to the main structure. It may require some care to make a good junction between the lower roof of the former with the higher one of the latter, unless the ridge of the one can be brought under the cornice or eaves of the other. Again, the union of the main and inferior structures should be so harmonized, by the use of certain string courses or lines, common to both, as to show that the two or more parts are component features of one whole, the extension of which is not so much that of connexion as continuity. Finally, it will be well to avoid the probability of future appended additions, as out-houses, lean-to's, &c.; and never to put off the consideration of wood and coal-houses, shoe and knife-houses, dust-holes and privies, until the mass of the building is up.

There is one particular necessity in every good house, which the young architect should consider from the very first. It is a necessity not often very successfully met; because it is rarely considered until too late for efficient management. Water-closets are generally so placed as to make it a very difficult matter for ladies and gentlemen to conceal from one another the more humiliating circumstances of their common nature. It may be, that we are in England too nice on this point; but it is nevertheless a point on which an architect is privileged to exert his ingenuity. So place a water-closet, that any one going in its direction, or returning, is not necessarily going to or coming from *it*. Secondly, let it be so located that its door cannot be seen from the hall, the stair-case, or any important part of the house where the inmates are likely to be passing. Avoid, under any circumstances, putting it at the end of a long passage. Be still more particular in so placing the closet that the operations of the occupant and the apparatus shall not audibly announce themselves to the sitters in the day-rooms, or the sleepers in the bed chambers. But, above all, let not the vicinity of the closet be made known by any offence to the nose of nice gentility. On this last most important matter, we would call particular attention to the following precautions. Avoid, if possible, placing the cess-pit within the building. See to the certain efficacy of the stench-trap at the foot of the soil-pipe. Let not the waste-pipe from the cistern enter the cess-pit without the water first passing through a trap which shall prevent the ascent of effluvia into the locality of the cistern. If the soil-pipe can be carried outside the wall, let it be so ; only take every care to prevent any of the pipes from being injured by frost. Let not the cistern be uncovered to the air, lest the mouths of the pipes, &c., be choked with leaves or other matter carried there by wind or rain. While on the subject of plumbers' work, let us impress upon our young practitioner its foremost importance, and the necessity of giving the fullest description of it. It is usually too much *generalized.* Always employ rolls and drips to unite the sheets of lead. Do not use solder where it can be avoided. Leave the lead free to expand and contract. Cover the gutters with raised boarding. Provide capacious receiving-boxes at the heads of water-pipes. Take every precaution to prevent leaves and rubbish from collecting in the boxes and choking the pipes ; and be equally careful to carry the water from the feet of the pipes immediately clear of the building and into the drains ; otherwise they will only prove most injurious to the very stability of the building by soaking the foundations. In constructing drains, have a close regard to the facility of cleansing them, especially where they unite with the pipes; and be equally careful in the supply of traps to prevent the progress of rats and vermin. It is too commonly supposed that workmen will have an eye to all these obvious necessities: but workmen might as well imagine that their tools will work of their own accord, as might architects conceive that workmen are to be trusted without accurate description and scrutinizing supervision. We thus mix up mere *practical* matters with matters of pure *taste*, as an example of the combined process which should ever be going on in the mind of the architect.

In connexion with the subject of drains, we should not forget to mention the frequent advisability of constructing a dry drain to preserve the face of the underground walling from damps; and as a matter of equal importance, the young architect will not forget the mischief of dry-rot, and the noisome exhalations of foul and stagnant air from beneath such ground-floor or basement rooms as have not a free ventilation beneath their joists, effected by apertures and gratings in the outer walls.

We have now disposed of the leading considerations which should be entertained by the young architect in forming his plans and elevations of the general carcase of a dwelling house, alluding to such paramount practical matters as are necessary to insure the comfort of its occupiers, without which all merits of architectural propriety and decorative beauty will be regarded as the mere impositions of taste to conceal defective convenience and careless construction. People whose tempers are disturbed by leaks, and offensive smells, by damps and smoky houses, or even by partial failures in design, will become proportionally blind to the numerous merits which may still remain; and the architect, at the moment of signing his last certificate, " that the contractor has fulfilled all his duties in the most complete and workmanlike manner," may be, in effect, signing the declaration of his own inefficiency, and, unconsciously, entering on a period of much trouble and perplexity, when he imagines the completion of a pleasing labor, which is to establish his professional competency and produce much future employment. To call his attention to the remaining numerous details of his work, the copious Stock Specification which forms the substantial worth of this volume will, we trust, be found sufficient; or, at least, sufficiently assistant, in conjunction with his own acquired knowledge and sagacity. A studious and repeated perusal of Bartholomew's "Practical Architecture," Part I., will supply all that is here omitted; and will afford not less information on the subject of the Beautiful than on that of the Constructive. We especially allude to the First Part; because we regard the Second as wanting in that arrangement and condensation which would have rendered its valuable materials more immediately available; and it is certainly to be regretted that Mr. Bartholomew did not, by his own more able industry, render unnecessary the attempt which is here made to supply the deficiency of his work. Far be it from the supposition of any one that this volume is intended as a *rival* to his. Our object is only to *co-operate* with him in facilitating the practical career of the young architect; and it would be most unjust in any writer, having the like aim, to omit the notice of Mr. Gwilt's very valuable Encyclopædia of architectural information. Wherever any of the principles of this book shall differ from those of Messrs. Gwilt and Bartholomew, it is only requested that the reader will instantly transfer his confidence to the monitorship of these gentlemen.

It will now be as well to afford a few hints as to the relative position of the architect and his employer. The former usually errs in giving to the other a credit for thoroughly understanding his drawings; while the latter equally errs in thinking that his architect is omniscient, not only in the general laws of design, but also in the particular fancies of individual patronage. Now the correction of the employer is out of the question. He must be taken as he is found; and the architect must then find out what he *is*, "hanging clogs on the nimbleness of his own soul, that his patron may go along with him." What the employer *says* is not invariably what he *means;* and he does not always think that he is bound to say *much* to a professor who is supposed to know *everything*. He gives vague ideas of form and size and arrangement, which the architect too hastily receives as positive instructions; and, the result proving wrong, he is abused for not having acted in correction instead of obedience.

Be cautious, then, in the first instance, of receiving, as law, the dimensions which are given for the required size of rooms. Show your employer an existing room of the form and size he describes, and learn that he means such a room. If you have not assured yourself of this, your troubles will begin before the walls are twelve inches above ground; for he will then declare that the room is much less than the model chosen, and will hardly believe it to be otherwise, in spite of the arithmetic which shall be conclusive that it is so. Nothing is more deceptive than the appearance of comparative smallness in the rooms of a building only plinth high.

Consider, secondly, that the mode of finishing rooms,—with a heavy, or light, cornice; a dado, or only a simple skirting; a plain, or a richly decorated, ceiling,—materially affects their apparent size; the space taken from the plain part of the walls and ceiling, being, in effect, equal to a diminution of actual capacity; or, at least, to an alteration of its proportions. The annexed figures will illustrate this fact. Seen in close proximity, their sizes are observed to be the same; but looked at in separate succession, fig. 1 will be called long

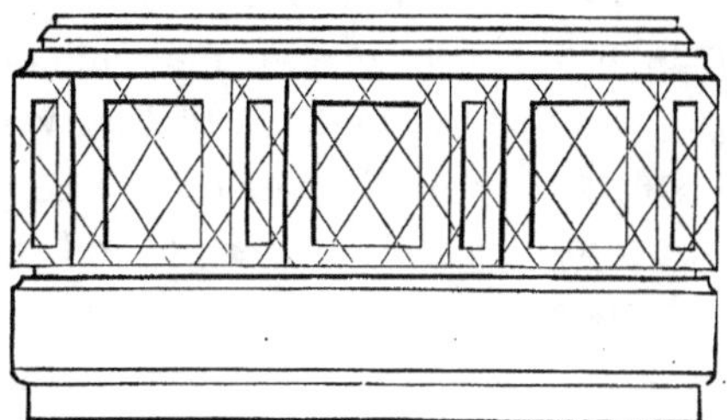

Fig. 1.

and low, fig. 2 spacious and high.

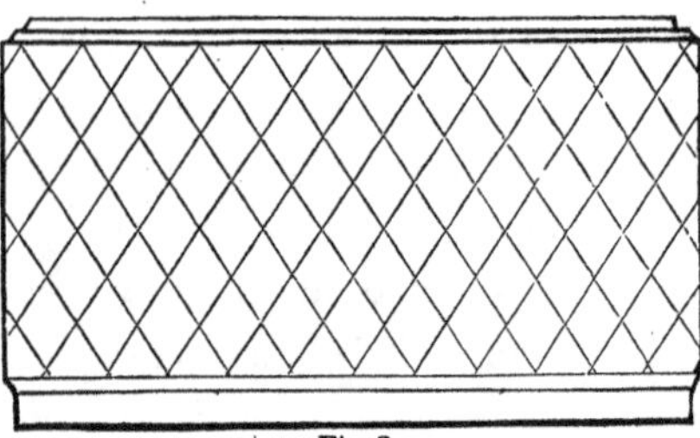
Fig. 2.

Having, therefore, satisfied your employer in *real* dimension, — a question touching only his carpet-room, table, and chairs,— you may disappoint him in the expression of *apparent* dimension, which is a question of optics.

The *expression* of relative sizes and proportions will, in fact, be the only certain assurance of the patron's complete approval; and, thoroughly to effect this, a differing altitude, in rooms, &c., of differing magnitudes in the same house, should be given where readily practicable. If, for instance, corridors of only six feet wide, lead to rooms of sixteen feet wide, and both be of the same height, the former will appear too narrow, the latter too low. Both will be advantaged by diminishing as much as may be the height of the corridor; and where the actual ceiling of the latter cannot (on account of the corresponding height of the doors or windows of both) be sufficiently lowered, a frieze, or entire entablature, with a higher skirting, or a dado, may so diminish the apparent height of the corridor as to give it seeming width, and preserve undiminished the height of the room. Here in fact is the legitimate use of false or pseudo-architecture; and there is no doubt that of two houses, the one well studied in these particulars, and the other not, the former will leave a general impression of spaciousness in all its rooms which in the latter will be wanting. Cornices will therefore be thrown flat on the ceiling; brought down upon the wall; with friezes; or complete entablatures

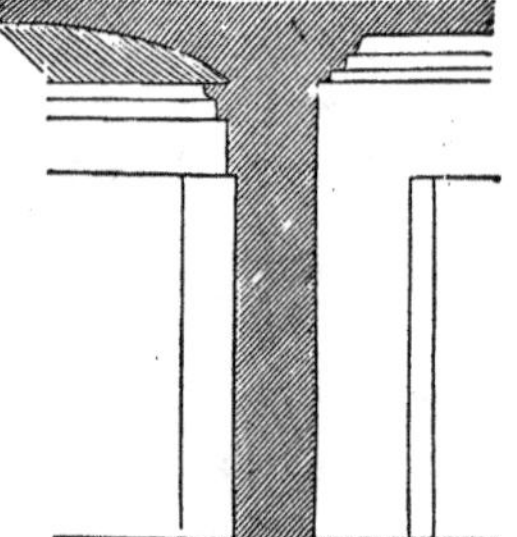

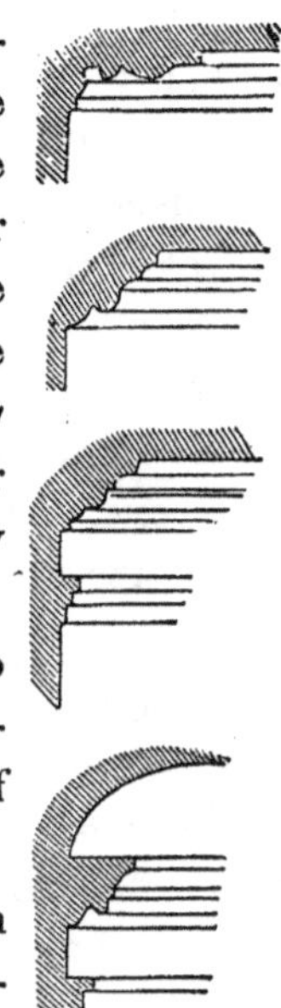

either immediately connected with the level ceiling; separated from it by a cove; or forming the imposts of a segment or circular ceiling,—as the rooms and passages shall be relatively higher or lower. It is not merely to please the eye of the critic that this is done. He will indeed have the double pleasure of seeing it, and of knowing *why* he sees it; but it is sufficient that your employer is well satisfied with the result, without any knowledge of the wherefore.

Another point of frequent disappointment to your employer is the width or height of the windows, and more particularly of the position of their sills in relation to the floor.

He may be pleased by their appearance in your elevations, but he may have such particular notions of his own as to their effect inside the rooms, that a material and costly alteration may subsequently increase the bill of extras and affect the beauty of your exterior. Be clear, then, in the beginning, whether sliding sashes or French casements are to be insisted on? Whether the sitting or other room windows are to reach or nearly reach the floor? or whether there are to be backs and elbows; and at what height the glazing is to commence? Forewarn him that French casements are, in this country, scarcely to be rendered weather-tight: that if they open outwards, they are liable to be dashed to pieces by the wind; if inward, they interfere with curtains and defy falling Venetian blinds. Again, if there are to be outer folding shutter blinds, your architraves or other dressings will be in the way; outer shutters, in short, are most hostile to decorative dressings. Lastly, venture not on the square attic window (a favorite with Palladian architects) without apprising your employer, that if it have sliding sashes it can only be two panes high, and therefore can only open one-half of its height—scarcely enough, perhaps, to admit your head and shoulders;—that such a sash is apt to catch and grow stubborn in opening; and that there will be very likely a large space of wall (which, however, may be relieved by an upward splay) above its soffit and the ceiling. Consider, further, that if it is to be so heightened as to admit of three panes, it will only be one-third of its height, unless another third be received into a casing in the thickness of the wall above, and that, then, there will be some difficulty in well hanging the upper sash, which will be only *one* pane high. In large bay, or triple windows, the management of the shutters should be considered even in the first sketch of your plan. They may be too wide to allow of the ordinary folding shutters in side boxings only; there may be objections to form additional boxings against the mullions; lifting shutters, from casings beneath the sill of the room floor, may be required. Leave not these considerations "for the future." Think of them at once. In domestic *Gothic* windows, especially, be careful to anticipate. Mullions and transomes of stone demand the greatest care in forming a weather-tight meeting with casements of metal; and mullions and transomes of wood will be tortured with alternations of heat and wet. They are fearful contrivances to catch the beat of weather, and to hold it when caught, till it bubbles through the sash or casement joints, and calls for the housemaid to bring pots and pans to catch the unwelcome stream. Are casements, or sashes, to be used? If the former, the framing will be *solid;* if the latter, hollow *cased.* Are the sashes to rise through the transomes? Are the casements to open inwards or outwards? Nothing may be easier to the architect than such a sketch of a Gothic front as will fascinate his employer's eye. Sharp and vigorous touches of the pencil, picturesquely showing the moulded recesses of a Tudor window, are readily done; but not so the contrivance of such working details as shall in execution preserve the pictorial and keep out the rain. Consider the cost of the long rod bolts, and other expensive articles of copper and metal, which the pelting of the storm will render imperative. If these "appliances" be not thought of at the first, your employer will surely regard them, in their subsequent adoption, as remedial *Extras* to make good radical defect. Our own perplexities in these particulars have been frequent and harassing, and we would put our younger brethren on their guard. Let them recollect, that, in a smart sketch, they draw out and sign a promissory note, which may require all the wealth of their practical attainment to pay. A gentleman, in employing an ARCHITECT, will not fail to consider that he *might* do without one; and it is, therefore, under the impression of something over and above what the BUILDER could do for him, that he incurs the expense of professional advice and assistance. The least he has a right to expect, is the value of the *artistical*, in addition to that of the *practical*; and he may reasonably expect yet more. Superiority of taste, and of ingenuity in arrangement, he will look for as a matter of course; and it must be admitted that he has also a right to superior knowledge in respect to the economical (and at the same time fully efficient) management of material and general construction. But he will frequently (and not with so much reason) look for more still, and be inclined to visit upon his Architect those failures in *particular* construction which only good workmen can insure, under the direction of the contracting Builder, and the supervision of an ever watchful Clerk of the Works, exclusively occupied on one job. It will be well, therefore, for the Architect at once to undeceive his employer in this last particular. He cannot be always present to see that the interior of the walls is well compacted with solid filling and sufficient mortar; that foundations and drains, which are concealed as soon as laid, have been executed in thorough obedience to his specifications; that every slate is properly nailed, and every piece of lead flashing inserted sufficiently in the masonry; that all the carpentry is thoroughly sound and seasoned; that all the joinery is properly "framed, glued, and blocked;" that the plastering has been mixed in the prescribed proportions, and efficiently worked up; that the flues are all of the full size and properly pargetted; that paving has been laid on a well-prepared bottom; in short, he cannot, during only the occasional visits of inspection which he engages to afford, see into those parts of the work which have, in the intervals, been concealed; nor can he anticipate those future deficiencies, either in work or material, which may not show themselves in any degree until some time after the occupation of the premises. He will have done much in observing, that all, which from time to time remains developed to him, is effected to his satisfaction; and his drawings and specifications will still remain, to justify, under any future chance of impeachment, their sufficiency as a means towards a satisfactory end. Even a contractor, however practically competent, cannot be always on the spot; and no merely ordinary foreman can be trusted in his stead,—because *if* he be so trustworthy, he is worthy of the double pay which will leave him an "ordinary foreman" no longer. When, therefore, an employer will not take upon himself the responsibility of trusting to the efficiency of the Contractor and his men, the Architect is bound to insist on the engagement of a well-tried Clerk of the Works. The author of these hints has suffered so much from a too ready desire to save his employer the charge of a constant supervisor, that he cannot too strongly urge upon those, whom he now addresses, the advisability of having a clear understanding with their patrons on this point.

To recur to a few matters of TASTE in the interior finishings of houses. We recommend the young architect to provide a good and varied supply of specimen drawings for the enrichments of cornices, ceilings, internal dressings and panellings of doors and windows; chimney-pieces, of marble, for sitting and best bed-rooms; of wood, combined with stone or marble, for bed-rooms; of wood, with slate slips, to keep the former from the heat of the fire; and of cheap simple chimney-pieces of Portland or slate, for kitchens, offices, and inferior rooms; designs for columned skreens, dividing a long sitting-room into two compartments, and supporting a partition wall, or stack of chimneys, in the rooms above; for columned or pilastered decorations for dining-room recesses; for staircase or other lanterns, with their cornices, and the enriched soffits round their openings in the main ceiling; for turned wood or cast iron, stair-balusters; for cast iron lights over entrance door transomes.

All these are matters in which the individual fancy of the architect, and the whim of his employer, may be more indulged than in those severer and more conventional features which constitute external architectural decoration and character; and the young professor, during the leisure of his yet only partially occupied time, may advantageously keep up his hand as a draughtsman, and invigorate his imagination as an artist, by studying them, and providing a series of such examples as will, hereafter at least, prove suggestive, if not ready at once for adoption. Employers can rarely see *what* they desire, unless they first see something *like* it. The slight sketches of these things which appear in small sections and elevations, or which are vaguely described in specifications, will merely serve as postponements of available consideration, and this will arrive at a period when you may regret not having entertained it before. Against a sketch or slight description, a contractor puts a low and unconsidered price; and when your working drawings are afterwards made out, he considers them as much beyond the thing intended, as the employer thinks them beneath it.

The economy of ornament is not so much shown in employing it only where most needed, as in sparingly employing it, with due relative proportion, in *every* place where it is needed at all. Thus, in all parts of a house which are seen in immediate and unconcealed connexion with the principal rooms, their relationship *to* those rooms should be marked. As an instance of prevailing defect in this particular, we may allude to the application of bold and handsome cornices to staircases and the ceilings of staircase landings, while the plastered soffit of the stairs forms a plain and mean looking junction with the face of the wall. You need not, it is true, continue the modillions of a landing cornice down the rake of the stair soffit to the floor; but you should unquestionably continue down it one or more of the upper mouldings of that cornice. White plastered soffits are not, in fact, the most suitable to a range of wainscot stairs. Plaster *expresses* stone; and no one would think of casing the ends, risers, and treads, of a flight of stone steps with wood. The soffit of a wooden flight of stairs should, therefore, either be formed of wood panelling, or of plaster, papered or painted in imitation of it: but, under any circumstances, forget not the raking moulding. Even when the stairs are of stone, with under-cut mouldings, we would still show the moulded work stopping short of the part of the stone inserted in the wall, forming the intervening part into a continuous raking line, and running under it the plaster moulding we have alluded to.

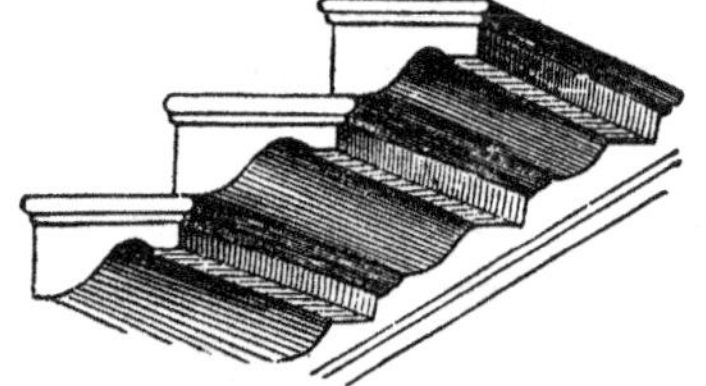

In allusion to a few matters of COMFORT and CONVENIENCE, we would hint at the virtue of being a match for the occasional violence of gusty weather, in so contriving that two doors shall be passed before you are fairly in the body of the house. Thus an enclosed porch will enable you to shut the outer or porch door, before the inner or passage door is opened. An entrance vestibule should, if possible, have only one outer door, and one inner door leading into the staircase or hall of common internal communication. The interception of thorough draughts cannot be too attentively considered. A range of doors, all opening one way, in a long passage with a window at each end, will often exhibit the very perfection of the evil ; and you may not expect your lady patroness to give much eulogy to the perspective of your corridor if she loses her cap in passing through it, and only gains in return a sore throat. The air that can quietly and courteously insinuate itself into rooms under the bottoms of the doors, in the chinks between the casements and rebates, and through the fire-place, is a welcome and necessary guest ; but when it takes to *slamming* doors, breaking windows, and carrying hearth-rugs up the chimney, it is a symptom of some great want of caution in the architect.

The best situation for fire-places in a large room is, unquestionably, in the centre of the longer side ; and, for doors, close to the extremity of the same. The worst position for doors is at the extremities of the walls at right angles to the fire-place side, looking directly over the length of the hearth. Where doors communicate between rooms, they will be best placed in that part of the partition walls nearest the window side and furthest from the fire. In smaller rooms, where there is scarcely sufficient room for a central fire-place, and *two* doors equidistant from it on the same side, it is often better to put the fire opening in the centre of the length between the one door and the end of the wall. It is not only more comfortable, but, where there is no projecting chimney breast, more sightly. Under some circumstances a perfect preservation of centrality may be preserved by the use of breaks or pilasters and ceiling beams, as the adjoined figure exemplifies.

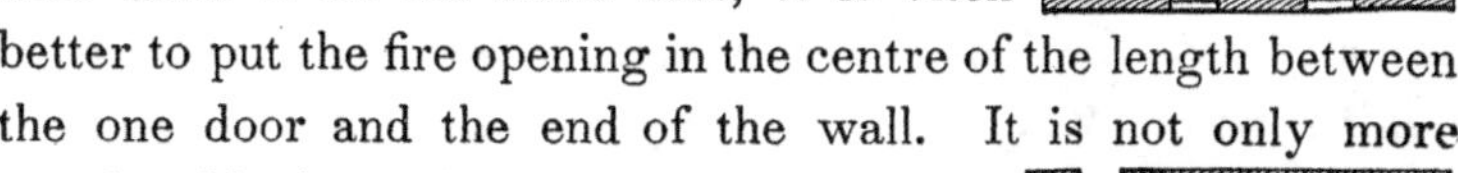

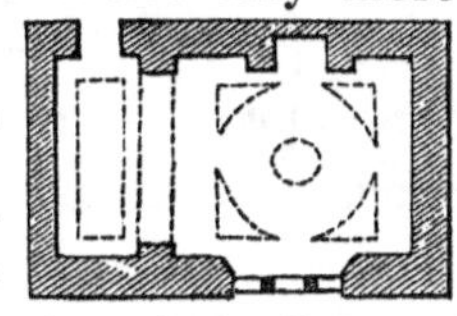

If any method of general warming and ventilation be

required, it will be for the architect to choose from the number of patents and practices in vogue, and to prepare for them in his first plans. An early conference with the patentees or professors of these methods should be of course secured, and their proposed operations duly provided for.

The perfection of kitchen and office comfort is, perhaps, a "consummation" more "devoutly to be wished" than any other; for all others are especially dependent on it. Expect no master or mistress to be happy, while a cook, housekeeper, and butler, are discontented. Keep the smell of the mutton fat, cabbage water, and chopped onions, out of the main house, for the sake of the hostess and her guests; but, for the united sake of all parties, make your kitchen, scullery, larder, store-room, and pantry, replete in all the sufficiency of space, fittings, and communication. Old servants may have accommodated themselves to old defects; but the success of new and better arrangements will, for a length of time, remain problematical. Your only chance is to flatter old servants by consultation. Learn from them the merits and demerits of their present accommodation; submit the result of your ingenuity, and of their exactions, to the upper house; and thence deduce a well-studied plan, to be again modified till you *think* both houses are satisfied. Forget not the cook's closet, the still-room, the china closet. Remember that, besides a larder for cooked meat, another for hung meat, and a salting-room, may be required. The dairy may be insufficient without a scalding-room and a churning-room. The butler's pantry may be incomplete without a separate glass-washing and plate-cleaning room, and a strong closet for the security of plate not in constant use. Enable the housekeeper to have an eye on the cook, and the means (by a sliding door) of communicating with the kitchen without necessarily going into it. Keep the servants' hall and back entrance out of the way of the operations and runnings to and fro during the bustle of dinner; but, at the same time, "handy" for a speedy advance to the front door of the main house. Remember, that a butler's satisfaction is improved by well-arranged cellars for beer, strong ale, wine in casks, and ditto in bins ; and that a master's comfort is enhanced by ready access to the said cellars from his own part of the building. Forget not, that it will be well if the brew-house is connected by pipes with the cellars ; and especially bear in mind that pipes of wine which are from 5 to 6 feet long have to go lengthwise down an inclined plane and through doorways into the cask cellar. A corking-room and a bottle-room follow of course. Let your coal and fuel stores be prompt for the supply of offices and main house, and consider that coals are of at least two qualities, and must exist divided. Let your gallantry think of pretty maids carrying coal-scuttles in their hands without bonnets on their heads, and provide covered ways for their benefit. To the boot and knife-house it may be well to add a brushing-room with a good stove in it, or a drying closet for wet clothes. Let the wash-house yield its cleansed linen readily to the laundry, and the laundry its mangled and ironed ditto to the linen-room. Consult propriety in keeping the maids and the men-servants in a state of respectful separation, with separate staircases to their respective dormitories. Let the housekeeper's and butler's sleeping-rooms respectively command those of the former.

Returning into the main house, we may mention the convenience of a waiting-room connected with the master's private room ; and again, connected with the latter, a fire-proof strong closet and a gun closet. A gentleman's bath and water-closet will be well added to this nest of conveniences : a second bath and closet for ladies being provided on the floor next above. On each floor a housemaid's closet will be most welcome, with a pipe from the great reservoir in the roof, to supply each with water for the bed-rooms. The convenience of a ready supply of water from one or more reservoirs (to be filled, when not supplied by the rain, with water ejected from the tank below by a force-pump) will be obvious. The water-closets, baths, butler's room, &c., will be jointly dependent on it. The matter of water, though mentioned late in this Essay, will be among the first things considered by the young architect, who has, no doubt, an adequate knowledge of well sinking and steining. It only remains to hint at the policy of providing ordinary closets wherever a recess in the masonry may allow it; for among the stronger impulses of woman is a passion for closets, shelves, rails, and pegs. To crown the ridge of this part of our fabric of hints, we simply allude to a good and well-located dinner-bell.

The usual accompaniment of a good house is a good stable building; and for many useful particulars on this subject, as well as in respect to farm buildings in general, we cannot do better than recommend Loudon's "Encyclopædia of Cottage, Farm, and Villa Architecture."

Let the young architect deny to *none* of his out-buildings the same amount of care which the main structure has had. All should show themselves to be of the same family. The stable court will often afford an opportunity for an advantageous display of simple and expressive Architecture. The interior of the quadrangle may exhibit the rough sketch of the more finished external façades, which will admit of much characteristic decoration. For instance, the entrance into the court forming the centre-piece of a range of stables is a most legitimate opportunity for adopting the general *form* of the Roman triumphal arch: and, in fact, as good and handsome stables are becoming, more and more, one of the signs of squirearchical importance, the young architect will take the subject into his best consideration. The following hints may be of service.

Space enough for a carriage to drive in, turn, and be backed easily into the coach-house: not less than thirty feet wide.

Large open porch before stable door for cleaning dirty horses in wet weather. ·Harness-room between the stable and coach-house, with an opening in the partition wall for an Arnott's stove, common to the coach-house and harness-room. It is most essential that both of these should be dry, and capable of being heated. Boxes not less than the width of two stalls; each stall and box having an efficient ventilating aperture close to the ceiling over the horse's head. In the loft over, avoid flat collar-beam roofs which thrust out the walls. The annexed is the ordinary roof adopted by the author. Let not your smallest stables be less than ten feet high to the under edge of the loft joists. Give larger stables one or two feet more.—Avail yourself of the additional air space afforded by the depth of joists, by having no plastered ceiling; but be careful that your floor boarding above is close, with ploughed and tongued joints. Let your stall-posts run up to take a head-piece to support the joists of the loft. If one side of your extreme stall be necessarily a *wooden* partition (which is not well), board it to the top: the kicking and movements of a restless horse will shake down plastering. In coach-houses, place guard stones, and form tram courses and stops, to prevent the wheels, &c., from rubbing against the walls and one another, and the backs of carriages from being injured against the back of the coach-house. Guard your door-posts with hard stone plinths to direct the wheels on being backed in. Seven feet clear space is ample for a carriage to pass through. Width of stables and depth of coach-houses not less than fifteen, commonly sixteen, and need not exceed eighteen feet. Entrance carriage-way into court not less than ten feet clear.

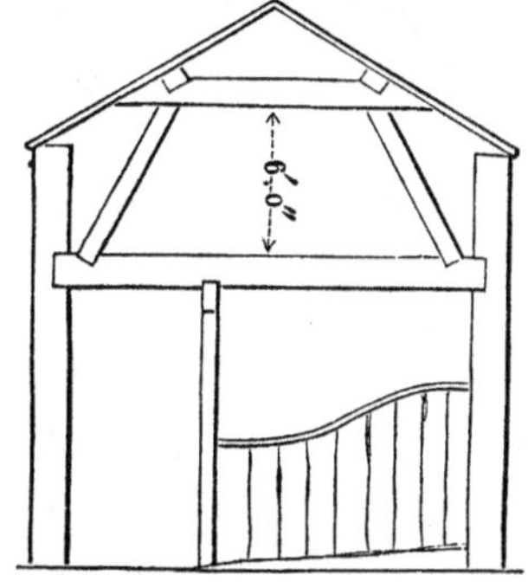

Gentlemen and their grooms differ in the ideas to which the following queries refer. The young architect will therefore inquire—General dimensions as to widths, depths, and heights? Are the stalls to have surface drainage to trickle into the open gutter at foot of stalls, as 1? or a central cess-pit and under-gutter, as 2? and are they to be flat-paved, or pitch-paved? (N.B. Be careful that the open gutter be not a trap to catch the hoof. It should be so wide and shallow as to prevent this danger, or be covered with a grating.) Are the rack and manger to be of wood, level, and near the ground, as 1? or one above the other, as 2? or of cast iron, and placed as 3? Is the hay to be thrown down from the loft into the rack, or brought to it from a store on the ground level? Is the corn to be in a chest below? or to be supplied into the stable by a trough connected with the corn store in the loft? (N.B. Case your corn chest with tinned sheet iron, or the rats and mice will work into it.) Is any portion of the loft to be employed for men's sleeping-rooms? If so, there must be regular stairs; otherwise a step-ladder may serve. Consider the position and provision of a door for admitting hay and corn into the loft. Is there to be a crane, or bracket with pulley, &c.? Agree upon the position of the dung-pit, as convenient for the removal of the dung to the gardens or fields. Is it to be so constructed and cemented as to hold liquid manure? Can you unite the sewerage of the house with that of the stables? (Do not conduct the water from the roof pipes and the surface of yard into the liquid manure tank.) Will the pebble stones of the vicinity afford

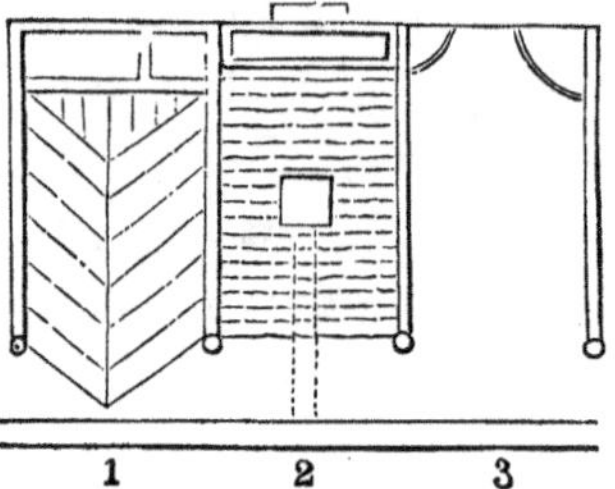

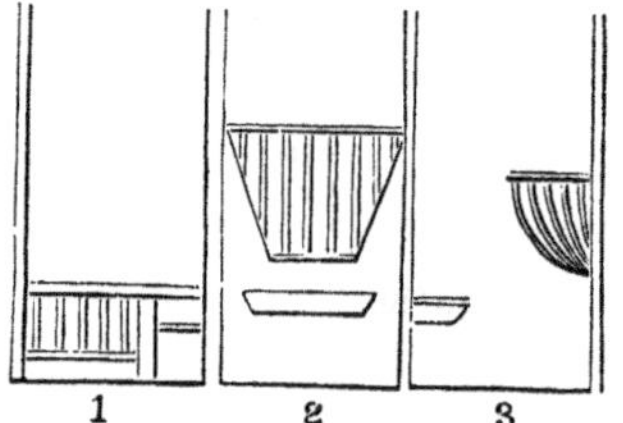

good paving? or must you procure granite or other spalls for it? Remember that the tread and kicking of horses will soon disturb it, if it be not well bedded, close set, and well rammed. Defects in this particular are of great annoyance. Is a clock tower required? a pigeon-house? a dog-kennel? Stable-privies will, of course, be placed near the dung-pit. Are any open sheds required? carpenter's shop? smithery? well? watering-tank? separate horse infirmary?

For more detailed information on these subjects, and for abundant instruction in regard to farm buildings, &c., we again refer to Mr. Loudon's publications.

A word on the subject of LODGES. They are too frequently more pretending in their architectural appearance than perfect in their internal comfort. A living-room and a little closet of a sleeping-room are crammed into a Portland stone case; and while the Greek order in its full external development emulates an Athenian Propyleum, there is little but *dis*-order within, from the lack of those absolute conveniences which even the humblest cottager cannot do without. To preserve in cleanly neatness the day-room (in which nobility itself sometimes takes shelter), and to prevent pots and pans from showing in the front of our Doric portico, there must be back rooms and back premises in reasonable sufficiency. The poor lodgekeeper is rarely admitted into those preparatory consultations which are open to the housekeeper, butler, and cook; and it therefore behooves the architect to be his especial advocate. A lodge, in fact, should be a little *house*, and not a little *temple*. There is not that difference between the lord of the mansion and the keeper of the gate that there is between a Christian and a house-dog. No MAN, who is in the service of his wealthier fellow, should live in a *kennel*, however smart its "complement extern." Occupy, then, that space which will allow of subdivision into room for sitting and sleeping in comfort; for stowage of food, crockery, and fuel; for cooking and cleansing, and other *necessary* matters. Give the lodgekeeper his well and pump, or, at least, his tank and filterer, that he may not be denied the luxury allowed by Teetotalism.

In respect to the *style*, we think the *principal* entrance lodge should be a fitting prologue to the "swelling act of the imperial" mansion: true to it, in architectural character, as the mansion portico to the mansion itself. In the secondary and other lodges or cottages, the caprice of a taste for variety may be indulged. The lodge at the opening of the grand avenue should assuredly be prophetical of the grand structure at the end of it; but there may well be, in other parts of the ground, the *Gothic* lodge, the *Italian* lodge, the *thatched* lodge, and the *Swiss cottage.* The strictest epic poem admits its episodes; and the different pictorial aspects of different situations on a gentleman's estate may be suggestive of differing architectural models.

In regard to PUBLIC BUILDINGS, it would be impossible, in a work of this limited extent, to give anything like the detailed instruction which we have ventured to afford in respect to domestic buildings. A few cautionary hints on the manner of dealing with BUILDING COMMITTEES will prove valuable.

We suppose a case.

You have, either by successful competition or immediate commission, obtained the opportunity of executing a church, or any other important structure, in which the opinions of a Board of Directors are to be collected and consulted. The most respectful attention, and the most penetrating efforts to discover the substance of those opinions, is, of course, your duty; and it is not impossible that you may succeed in obtaining some manageable stuff to mould into form; but, under any circumstances, it is advisable you should "oppose your *patience*" to their perplexities, and "arm yourself with a quietness of spirit to meet the probable tyranny of theirs." That they may have chosen *your* plan as the best of many, or that they may have approved your design on general grounds, must not leave you to imagine that the "working drawings" are all you have now to prepare, and the cares of uninterrupted supervision the only ones you have to encounter; since all the raw ideas of improvement, which may successively and suddenly suggest themselves to the various members of the Committee, must be disposed of, either by the labor of incorporating them with your own, or by long and weighty arguments to prove them "frivolous"—if not "vexatious." Take pains, then, to explain your drawings fully before full Committee, and to get the signature of the Chairman attached to them before you proceed with the executive. Take especial care that the plans, to which your first estimate had reference, be preserved; and that you obey no injunctions for increasing or altering those plans, without first giving in writing (of which you have a copy) a statement of the addition or deviation which will be thereby occasioned in the cost. Improvements will be constantly desired by unauthorized authority, of which chairmanship takes no current note; and, in the end, memory will only recognise the architect's original estimate.

Of course your alterations and additions will be shown in a new set of drawings; the original set being put aside with its proper estimate. Be urgent in again and again begging the fullest consideration of your drawings and specifications before you go to public tender, impressing upon the Committee the impolicy of making alterations after a tender has been accepted. Make it, however, a condition with persons competing, that the one whose tender is accepted shall give in his detailed quantities and prices. Before it is accepted, require him to abide by any mistakes he may have made in the former, and to allow of any additions or reductions, at their full amount of quantity, and at the prices which he now gives in. It is *his* business to see that the quantities are sufficient; *yours*, that the prices are not too high.

It may be, on the reception of his tender, that there appear reasons for reducing or augmenting the work. If, however, this be not very important in its amount, it may not be necessary to make fresh drawings, &c., as the contract may be concluded in reference to those already prepared, the deviations being shown in making the *working* drawings, being only careful, that before the works commence, the difference of cost be regularly recorded by the Treasurer, and that the order for proceeding be signed by the Chairman.

We may here remark on the advisability of an architect's being very clear in his notice to contractors, and in his instructions to the lawyer who draws up the contract. As a suggestion for the former we submit the following :

"To Builders, and others. Persons willing to contract for the erection of a ——— at ———, in the parish of ———, county of ———, may inspect the drawings and specifications at ———, from ——— the ——— day of ——— until ——— the ——— day of ——— now next ensuing. Tenders to be given in not later than ——— o'clock on ——— the ———. The advertisers do not engage to take the lowest tender ; nor will any be accepted unless the character, means, and sureties of the person offering it be satisfactory, and the amount of the tender within a certain sum. All further particulars or explanation will be given by the Architect at his office ——— ———."

Dated ——— Signed

In addition to this, many further cautions and intimations may be necessary, or, at least, advisable ; but these may be confined to the architect's office, or the room where the drawings are deposited : and it may be also urged, that all the parties tendering be required to put down their questions on a paper to which all shall have access, so that the replies attached, shall, by all, be seen : the object being, that, in fairness, all may understand the architect's intention alike. State how the legal expenses are to be borne.

As lawyers invariably differ in their way of wording an

agreement, an architect need be cautious how he ventures to act without their assistance. It is the author's practice to submit to the legal adviser of his employer a printed form, such as experience has enabled him to prepare. It has been often adopted at once: but still he ventures no further than to give its general substance, devoid of legal technicality.

"John Stokes, of ———, in the parish of ———, in the county of ———, having determined to erect a ——— at ———, in the parish of ———, county of ———, according to the drawings and specifications prepared by George Wightwick, Architect; and William Styles, of ———, in the parish of ———, in the county of ———, Builder, being willing to contract for the execution of the works, the said Styles agrees for the sum of £—— to perform them in a complete and workmanlike manner, agreeably, not only with the *letter* of the specification, and in conformity with the drawings *now given*, but also with the full *intention* of the specification, and conformably with other *future drawings* implied by the present, to the satisfaction of the Architect of the said Stokes; it being understood that Stokes will have the right of making any alterations or additions without vitiating the contract, and that the difference in the cost, so occasioned, shall be estimated by his Architect: That, in the event of the Contractor's bankruptcy, or of his failing to proceed satisfactorily, either as it regards time, materials, or workmanship, his employer shall be at liberty to employ other workmen, and to pay them out of the money which may yet remain unpaid to the Contractor, who will acknowledge that the amount of money he may have received before his bankruptcy is to be regarded as full payment for all the work he has done, as well as for all the materials, &c., which may be on the premises at the time; and that if such remaining money and materials are insufficient, the residue must be paid on demand out of the bankrupt's estate: that no money shall be at any time paid, except under the Architect's certificate that the works have been done satisfactorily; and that the Contractor, under certain penalties, shall bind himself to complete the works on or before the — day of ———, unless the Architect shall justify delay: that at certain stated periods of the work the Contractor shall receive money to the amount of two-thirds (or three-fourths) the value of work done, as the Architect shall estimate it, and that the residue one-third (or one-fourth) shall be paid within —— months after the completion of the works, provided no defects of workmanship or materials shall have shown themselves in that time; such defects to be remedied by the Contractor before it *be* paid."

We need hardly caution the young architect, before he gives a certificate, to be very scrutinizing in valuing the executed work *according to the proportional quantity*, or rather, with reference to the retention of a sum assuredly adequate to complete the building in the event of the contractor's failure. Bodies of men acting for the public have but little compassion for errors of judgment—still less of arithmetic. It is here that the *detailed tender* is of value. Try it, however, before you trust to it, and learn by the trial how to treat it in justice to yourself. Is it hard in an architect to bind a builder to his deficiencies of quantity or price? It is equally hard upon *himself;* for *he receives his per centage only on the amount of the deficient estimate!* It is a point of interest, *and honor*, in the contractor to take care that he has a proper price: it is a point of *honor only* in the architect—and *against his interest*—to see that the contractor keeps to his price, though it be too low. The position which an architect occupies relatively to his employer and the contractor is often very painful; and the very possible conclusion of a rupture with one, or the dissatisfaction of both, should so constantly be borne in mind, as to prevent too liberal a construction of the contract on the one hand, and too limited a one on the other. There is a natural tendency in all young and ardent minds to trust to the generosity of their patrons, the liberal intentions of their builders, and the favor of circumstances; and it is therefore the more necessary to impress upon the mind of the directing professor, that the patron and the contractor are equally trustful in the acuteness of the architect's foresight, and in the clearness of his intentions. It is well to insert in the contract such a "saving clause" as the following:—

"And the Contractor doth hereby admit that the said specifications and drawings are all-sufficient for the substantial and efficient erection of the buildings, &c.;"—

but it will be worse than useless, unless the architect, in the event of a dispute, is enabled to show and to prove that they really *are* so. A builder may justly conceive, that what *he* understands is what *you* mean; and he therefore unhesitatingly signs the admission you require. Be careful, then, that you do not wrong him by such vague clauses, as may, in truth, be little more than concealments of your own practical deficiencies.

With this we conclude our series of miscellaneous Hints, and proceed in an attempt to facilitate the operations of the young Architect in drawing his attention to such a methodical arrangement of practical detail as may enable him the more assuredly to perfect that most important of all means towards a "binding contract,"—a complete SPECIFICATION.

Only let him remember, that we profess to aid his experience, and not to supply his ignorance. Credit is given to him for much knowledge already acquired in the office of his former master; and our mere intention is to co-operate with that, to the relief of his labor, and the assistance of his yet unpractised responsibility.

PART IV.

MODEL SPECIFICATION.

INDEX.

RUBBLE MASONRY, WITH BRICK MINGLED.

		No
Facing.	Random coursed	51
	Regular coursed	52
	Trimmed and coursed	53
Arched soffits.	Trimmed rough—common brick—neat hammer-dressed—gauged—skew-back	54
Reveals.	Trimmed rough—common brick—neat dressed . . .	55
Arches.	Rough—counter-arches—relieving arches	56
	Inverted arches	15
Brick facing.	If any ? see	16
Projections, &c.	Corbellings—strings—fascias—cornices, &c, . . .	59
Fire openings, flues and chimney stacks		60
Coping.	Rough. No. 61. Rough, cemented	62
	Tile, or brick on edge coping	20
Bedding timber and stone-work—pointing round door and window frames —backing-up, &c.		63
Dwarf walling		64
Brick-nogging		65
Paving.	If of brick, No. 24. If tile, 25. If clinker . . .	26
Vaults.	Plain—groined—skew-backs—spandrils, &c. . . .	66
Lime whiting		32
Iron hoop bonding		33
Extra rubble-work and party-walls		67
Drainage, &c.	Cess-pit—barrel-drain—funnels—minor drains—dip-traps —main drain—soil-pit—dry area and tank—ventilation —jobbing	43 44 68
Rough stone-work built into masonry		70
Wrought stone work built into masonry		71
Rubble and brick-work to portico Ditto ditto to arcade	See note following No. 125.	

STONE CUTTING,

GENERALLY APPLICABLE EITHER TO GRECIAN, ITALIAN, OR GOTHIC WORK.

Steps.	Common door steps	72
	Common stair flights	73
	Better stair flights	74
	Stairs of paving stone	75
	Door steps of better quality	76
	Handsome stair flights with flat soffits	77
	Superior stair flights, with moulded soffits	78
	Stone steps, with iron risers	79

MISCELLANEOUS.

No.

SLATING.

TILING.

PLASTER AND CEMENT WORK.

	No.
Two coats common and one Abertthaw, on rubble	188
One coat ditto and two ditto ditto	189
Aberthaw, on brick	190
Cement or Aberthaw moulded work	191
	192
	193
	194
	195
	196
	197
	198
	199

CARPENTERS' WORK.

Inclosures	200
Shoring and old material	201
Piling and planking	202
Sundries	203
Bond and lintels	204
Story-posts	205
Bressummers	206
Quarter partitions	207
Ground joists	208
Common joisting	209
Binders and girders	210
Single-framed floors	211
Double-framed floors	212
Floor trusses	213
Cross straining	214
Ceiling battens	215
Flats	216
Lanterns	217
Roofs, Italian	218
Ditto Gothic	219
Dormer doors and windows	220
Boarding and battening for lead and slates	221
Open roof, Gothic	222
Curb roof	223
Garrets	224
Ceiling floors	225
Projecting eaves	226

JOINERS' WORK.

IRON AND METAL WORK.

PLUMBERS' WORK.

Specification of Works to be done in the construction of . . . . agreeably to the Drawings herewith furnished, and numbered 1 *to . . . inclusive.*

No. 1. Notice to local authorities. To give to the local Commissioners and Surveyors, &c., all requisite notices; to obtain all official licenses for temporary obstructions, inclosures, openings into common sewers, water-pipes, &c.; **Payment of fees.** and to pay all proper and legal fees and charges to public officers and neighboring proprietors, making good any damage occasioned to adjoining premises, and keeping up lights &c., required by night. **Protective inclosures.** Construct proper inclosures and fences for the protection and convenience of the public during the progress of the works; **Restoration of pavements.** and perfectly reinstate pavements, &c., to the perfect satisfaction of the Town Surveyors.

Clerk of the Works' office. An office for Clerk of the Works, with fire-place and flue of brick or masonry (see 200).

No. 2. Removal and shoring. Carefully take down the old buildings, effectually shoring up as may be necessary the adjoining properties; **Old materials.** and entirely remove the old materials, rubbish, &c., to the satisfaction of all parties. The old materials to become the property of the Contractor, who shall be allowed to re-employ only such portions thereof as the Architect under his handwriting shall permit.

No. 3. Clearing, excavating, refilling. Clear away all rock, soil, or rubbish, necessary to leave the site of the intended building clear and unincumbered; and excavate for basement story, areas, footings of walls, cess-pits, drains, tanks, vaults, &c., as shown by drawings. Properly refill, ram down, and level as required; and remove all superfluous matter excavated, to the satisfaction of all parties.

No. 4. Drainage of the site before building. Bale out, draw off, pump away, and remove all water and soil which may come into the excavations from springs, currents, drains, cess-pools, rain, or otherwise; and effectually complete the drainage of the excavations and footings before any masonry or brick-work be carried up. Shore up ground as required.

No. 5. Underpinning. Underpin in the most careful manner all walls, partitions, or buildings, surrounding the site of the intended new buildings, in any way endangered by the excavations of the latter.

No. 6. Trenches for footings. Make perfectly level, and hard, the bed of all trenches for footings; and consolidate the earth about the same, and against all walls, drains, pits, &c. The depth of the footings to be contracted for, as shown by the drawings. Should a less depth be admissible, or a greater depth be required, the deviation will be made, under the written permission of the Architect, and accounted for accordingly. [The depth of all trenches for walls and piers in the Northern States should not be less than three and a half feet, and in heavy soils four feet—to prevent upheaval by the action of frost.—Ed.]

No. 7. Artificial levels for pavements, and ground-making round building. To provide, bring in, spread over, and well ram and consolidate, any dry hard ground or rubbish which may be necessary to form the proper level for internal pavements, or paving of courts, areas, pits, &c.; or which may be required to raise the ground level to the lines shown on elevations or sections: the said made ground to extend . . . . feet from the fronts, and thence to fall to the natural, or now existing, surface, in an angle of . . degrees.

No. 8. Well digging and building. To dig a well, in the situation marked on plan, four feet diameter, and . . . feet deep below the level of . . . . The same to be properly steined round with . . . . and domed over with . . . .

No. 9. Concrete foundation. To make an artificial foundation for (either certain parts of, or) the entire building, ... feet in width, and . . . feet in depth; the same to be composed of one part of the best fresh quick stone lime, beaten to fine powder, and six parts of unscreened gravel (or fine and coarse stone ballast), mixed thoroughly with each other in small quantities at a time, the lime being moderately slacked with water at the moment of admixture; and the concrete, when properly compounded, and yet hot, to be thrown from an elevation of not less than ten feet into the trenches, where it will form in layers of six inches deep, to be repeated one above the other, until the full depth of the required substratum is attained. [The importance of *concrete* foundations is too little known or attended to in the United States. The settling and cracking, common in so many buildings, the foundations of which are directly laid in loose or unsuitable sub-soils, would be entirely prevented by simply forming a concrete base for the usual foundation walls.—ED.]

No. 10. Piling and planking. To make an artificial foundation for (either certain parts of, or) the footings of entire building, with sound fir piles, . . . feet long, . . . inches square, pointed with iron, and hooped with ditto; each pile to be firmly driven by means of a proper apparatus; the relative situation and distance of the piles, as shown by adjoining figured sketch. Sleepers ″ × ″ over each transverse row of piles, and . . . . planking . . . . inches thick; the whole properly spiked, &c., &c.

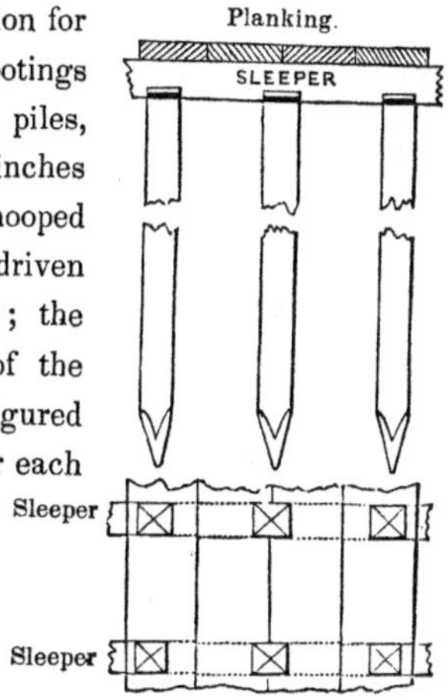

No. 11. Indents. To cut and parget in the old brick-work perpendicular indents to receive the new work, aud make good the disturbance in the old work occasioned thereby.

No. 12. Brick-work. The whole of the work, shown by . . . . tint on plans and sections, to be constructed with . . . . . . bricks,

General clause. laid in English bond; the said bricks to be the best of their kind, hard-burnt, square, and perfectly sound; laid in mortar

Mortar, &c. compounded of one-third well-burnt stone lime, and two-thirds of clean sharp sand, free from salt, well beaten and worked up together. No four courses to rise more than one inch beyond the collected height of the bricks. Every course to be filled in and fully flushed up with mortar, and every second (or third

Grouting. course) to be grouted with liquid mortar of hot lime and sand.

Footings, &c. See also No. 69. The footings and walls to be of the varying thicknesses and heights figured on the drawings; and no variation to be made between the outside work and inside work, except that the work intended to be plastered is to have the joints thereof left rough. (See 50.) [When a brick wall is to be plastered or covered with cement externally, the best mode is to lay the outside course of bricks with the mortar not brought out to a flush or struck joint, but laying back half an inch or more. This enables the cement to take a much firmer hold, much in the same way as common plastering upon laths.—Ed.]

No. 13. Brick. Common face pointing. Gauged and other arches, &c.

The visible exterior of walls above ground to be finished with a neat flat ruled joint (see 51); and all front windows and . . . . . . to have the best gauged arches, abutting on proper skew-backs, the soffits and reveals being 9 or 4½ inches deep. All other outer openings to have plain (and slightly cambered) arches closely set and tuck-pointed.

No. 14. Brick rough arches.

Turn rough arches and counter-arches wherever practicable, through the entire thickness of walls, except where it may be inexpedient to show them externally (in which case they will be concealed by four-inch facing), and construct nine or four-inch relieving

Relieving arches, &c. arches, over all lintels or bressummers, as sketch.

No. 15. Inverted arches, &c.

Inverted arches, the whole thickness of walls, under (—external openings,—chimney openings,—and other opening,—from pier to pier,—or) such openings (beneath the ground level) as are shown to have them on the drawings.

No. 16. Brick facing.

To face the visible exterior of the walls of the . . . . . with . . . . . . facing bricks of uniform color, properly bonded into back-work, and finished with a neat flat ruled joint.

No. 17. Brick strings and cutting. Properly form the string courses, fascias, pilasters, cornices, breaks, recesses, &c., shown by drawings (cutting and rubbing such of the work as may be moulded), (and neatly splaying angles, plinths, &c.).

No. 18. Brick fire-places, flues, stacks, &c. Properly form all fire openings, with camber arches over the same; and trimmer arches where required for front hearths. Carefully gather in the chimney throats, and carry up flues of not less than fourteen inches square in the clear; well pargetted. The stacks to be carried above roof to the heights shown in drawings, with salient courses, &c.; and properly fix the chimney tops hereafter described.

No. 19. Chimney bars. Chimney bars of wrought iron, $2\frac{1}{2}'' \times \frac{1}{2}''$, and 18″ longer than chimney opening, properly corked at the ends.

No. 20. Tile coping on brick, or Brick on edge. The walls of . . . . . to be finished with a top course of brick on edge (and coped with double plain tile cresting), set in and jointed with new Roman cement and clean sand mixed in equal proportions.

No. 21. Bedding, pointing, and backing. To bed in mortar all the bond timber, plates, lintels, wood bricks, templates, stone and other work requiring to be set in the { masonry / brick-work }. To bed in and point round with lime and hair mortar all door and window frames, and back up and fill in with solid { masonry / brick-work } all stone and iron-work demanding it. **Fixing Grates, &c.** Coppers, stoves, and grates, to be properly set with fire-bricks.

No. 22. Dwarf masonry or brick-work. Build all dwarf walls, piers, &c., necessary to receive sills of partitions and sleepers or joists of ground floor, as shown on plans. (Qy. *Cement* to upper courses.)

No. 23. Bricknogging. Bricknog all partitions which are marked on plans with a red hatching, thus:

No. 24. Brick paving. Pave the . . . . with hard . . . . bricks laid (flat, or on edge, as the case may allow) in mortar; and grout between the joints with liquid mortar. The bricks to be laid according to pattern here sketched, on a good and firm bottom previously prepared.

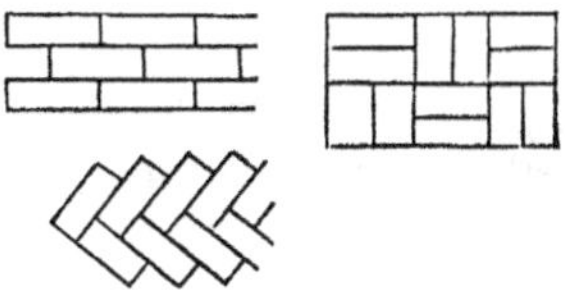

No. 25.
Tile paving, &c.

Pave the . . . . . with 12″ (red or white paving tiles) laid (square or anglewise) (either of *one* color or *both*, alternating) in mortar upon full 3″ deep of (fine coal ashes, dry brick, stone rubbish or lime core) bedding; and the joints thereof pointed with cement.

No. 26.
Clinker paving.

Pave the (stables, &c.) . . . . . with real Dutch imported clinkers of approved sample, laid herring-bone fashion upon coarse gravel 6″ deep, and grouted three times over completely with stone lime and sand. The paving to be laid with proper currents, &c. (every stall of stable to be groined).

No. 27.
Vaults of brickwork or r° masonry.

Construct over the . . . . . (pointed, segment, or semicircular, or elliptical) vaults of { r° masonry 12 / brick-work 9 } inches thick. The spandrils being filled to within 9″ of the crown of vaulting with { rubble / brick-bats } grouted in liquid mortar.

No. 28.
Groined vaults of brick-work or r° masonry.

Construct over the . . . . arched and groined vaultings, as drawings (with the groin points [if brick] accurately cut to a regular arris), and the spandrils filled with { r° masonry / brick-work } up to the internal crown of the vault. The whole to be completely grouted with hot liquid mortar; and, after the removal of centering, the whole to be neatly pointed.

No. 29.
Corbelled skew-backs.

The skew-backs of vaults to be formed by a corbelling (as C in adjoining sketch), so that the arch encroach not upon the main substance of the piers or springing walls.

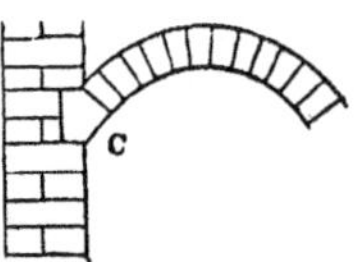

No. 30.
Concrete spandrils.

Construct vaults, &c., &c., &c., and fill up spandrils with concrete.

No. 31.
Vaults cemented outside.

Construct vaults, &c., and coat the outside of vaults and walls with Parker's cement ¾″ thick.

No. 32.
Lime whiting.

Stop and lime-whiten twice the . . . .

No. 33. Iron hooping. To employ . . . cwt. of iron hooping as may be directed, as a bond for the brick-work.

No. 34. Extra brick-work or rubble. Allow for . . { perch of extra rubble work / rod of extra brick-work } to be used, or not, as shall appear necessary, and accounted for accordingly.

No. 35. Party-wall. Party-walls. (Make arrangements with Contractor and adjoining Proprietors.)

No. 36. Cess-pit of brick, or masonry To construct, where shown on plan, a cess-pool, ′ ″ internal diameter, and ′ ″ from the bottom to the springing of (arched or domed) top. The same to be steined round, and vaulted with (4″ brick-work, or good compact rubble masonry), closely pitch-paved, and lined with Roman cement up to the springing of vault. A man-hole 20″ diameter to be left in the top; the same to be covered in with a (Yorkshire, Purbeck, or granite) stone having a strong iron ring therein. Attend Plumber in the admission of water-closet pipes.

No. 37. Brick-barrel drain. Construct a barrel-drain of 4″ brick-work, having a clear bore of inches, and the lower inside half to be stuccoed with pure quick Parker's cement. The same to extend from . . . . to . . . . .

No. 38. Dip-traps. Construct dip-traps where shown on plan; the same to be rendered water-tight with cement; and provide and fix sink stones over the same. [These dip-traps are indispensably necessary in all good drains, both to prevent the rise of smells and the passage of rats. See figure added. Ed.]

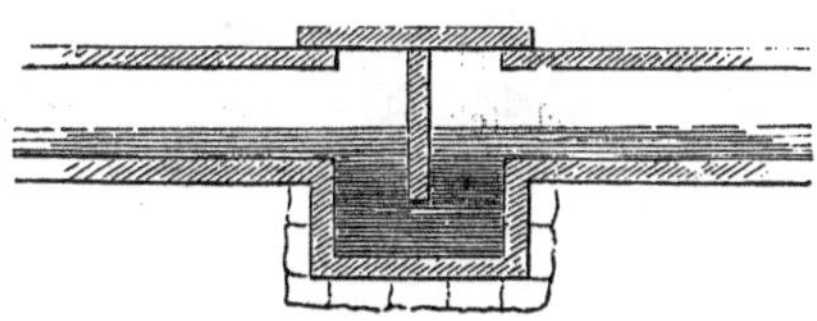

No. 39. Privy drain. Put from privy to drain a large and complete brick funnel; or form small trap cess-pit under the same, cemented to hold water, and brick barrel-drain ″ diameter from thence into larger drain.

No. 40. Minor drains.

Construct with { brick and tile, or brick only, or otherwise as sketch, } and of inches clear diameter, the several minor drains shown on plan, forming dip-traps where shown, and provide and fix sink stones over the same. (Qy. if only common mortar? laid in cement? lined with cement? brick and tile or brick only, or —)

No. 41. Brick funnels.

Form at the feet of soil pipes, waste pipes, and rain water pipes, brick funnels, set in Parker's cement.

No. 42. Drain pipes.

Lay, from the . . . . to the . . . . a drain of strong earthen pipes " diameter clear; and ditto of " diameter from the . . . . into the . . . .

No. 43. Drain of rubble, &c.

Construct, and continue, from the . . . to the . . . a drain " by " formed of good close rubble masonry at sides, slate bottom, and strong cover stone. The whole well bedded in mortar. (Qy. need a *portion* of it be lined with cement?)

No. 44. Main drain of brick or rubble.

Construct, and continue, from the . . . to the . . . . a main drain of (brick, or good rubble masonry in mortar) the form and size shown and figured in the annexed sketch. (Qy. whether, if of rubble, any part may be laid dry?)

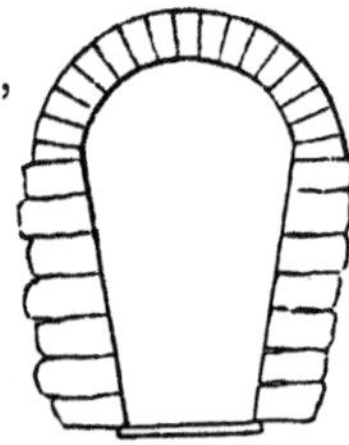

No. 45. Soil or dung-pit.

Construct a soil or dung-pit, &c., &c. Describe its size, form, material, and what drains it is to receive: whether open; with parapet? arched; with man-hole, &c.? or if covered with slate or stone slabs? whether lined (in part, or wholly) with cement, to hold liquid manure?

No. 46. Dry area of brick or rubble, &c. Form a dry area round the walls of . . (as shown on drawings), of (brick, or stone rubble-work), and of the sectional form and size shown and figured in the annexed sketch; the same to be (covered with flat stone, or arched with brick or rubble). Man-holes where shown on drawings; and provide and fix stone curb and gratings of iron therein, 20″ square. The bottom to have a fall to the drain, and to be pitch-paved.

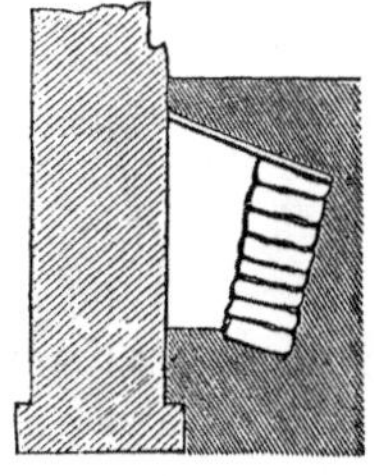

No. 47. Water tank, brick or rubble. Construct a water-tank below the floor of . . . . . as shown on plan, and of the sectional form and size here shown and figured. The same to be covered with a semicircular 4″ brick arch, having a man-hole, with stone therein, 20″ diameter, and iron ring. The sides to be of ″ (rubble or brick-work), the bottom of (ditto), and forming an inverted segment. The ground outside the sides and below the bottom to be thoroughly rammed and consolidated; the outside of said sides and bottom to be laid against a clayed backing, and the inside to be lined with fresh Parker's cement.

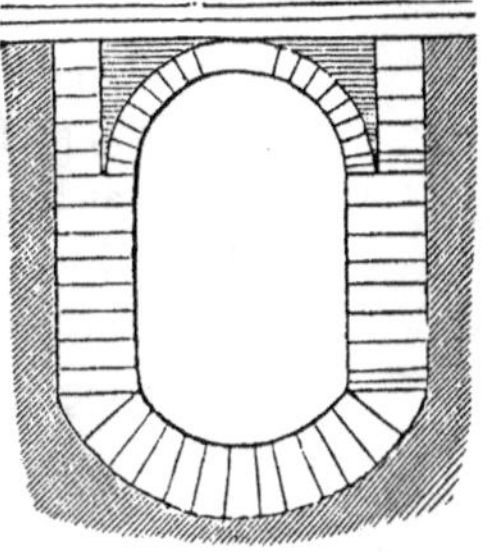

No. 48. Ventilation. Leave proper and sufficient openings for ventilating under the joists of ground floor, and provide and fix neat gratings in said openings. Form air flues, where shown, in thickness of walls.

No. 49. Jobbing, &c. Attend upon the Stone-masons, Carpenters, Plumbers, and Smith, aiding, and making good after them, and to perform all jobbing necessary to the perfect completion of the works.

No. 49½. Brick fittings. Half-brick piers to stone or slate shelves of cellar, dairy, larder, &c. (See 148.)

No. 50. Rubble masonry. The whole of the work, shown by . . . tint, on plans and sections, to be constructed of good { lime-stone, slate, or other } rubble masonry, **Mortar.** properly bedded in mortar, compounded of one-third well-burnt stone lime, and two-thirds of clean sharp sand, free from **Footings. (See also No. 69.)** salt, well beaten and worked up together. The footings of walls (see No. 69) to be formed of large flat stones (having their length not less than the width of the masonry above), laid transversely, as shown by sketch, A being

Bond & quoins. the footing stone. A sufficiency of bond stones, as B B B in the annexed figure (having an excess of *length*, and *not* of *height*), at all quoins and where else required to bind the work, and insure its uniform compactness, especial care being taken to make the walls of equal solidity all through by well filling the inner part **Grouting.** with small stones and mortar; and the work to be grouted with hot lime and sand at every rise of . . . inches. The stones to be bedded as found in the quarry. The walling to be carried up, and preserved, both vertically and horizontally true, and of the varying heights and thicknesses shown or figured on the drawings.

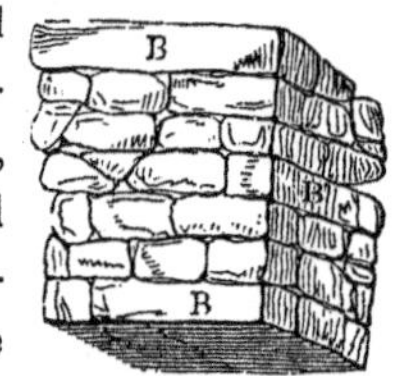

No. 51. Random coursed facing. The visible exterior of walls above ground to be finished in neat random coursed-work, the stones being hammer-dressed to a fair surface and neat joint, and well pointed.

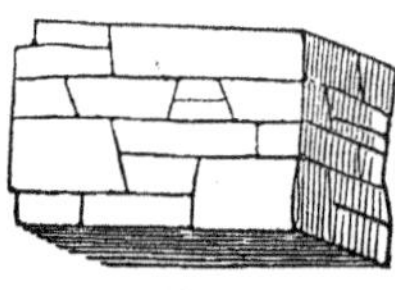

No. 52. Regular coursed facing. The visible exterior of walls above ground to be finished in neat and regular coursed-work; no course to be more than . . inches, nor less than . . inches high; hammer-dressed to a fair surface; the joints to be close, and true, both vertically aud horizontally, and pointed with Aberthaw mortar.

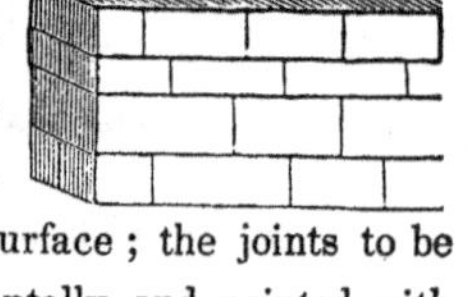

No. 53. Trimmed and coursed facing. The visible exterior of the . . . walls above ground to be faced with a neatly trimmed ashlaring of . . . . stone,

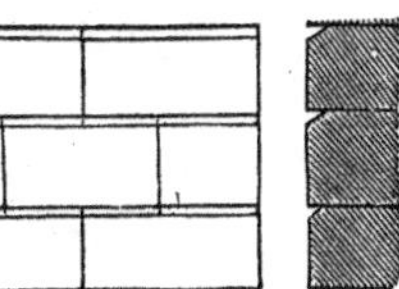

in courses of equal height (not less than inches, nor more than inches. The vertical joints tooled close, and the horizontal joints bevelled ('' by '') so as to throw the water from the top of each course, and pointed with (qy. Aberthaw ?) a neat flat ruled joint. (Qy. should this ashlaring be *bedded* and *backed* with Abertha\w ?)

No. 54. Arched soffits. All the . . . openings to have—(trimmed { segment / semicircular } rough arches)—(good common brick arches)—(neatly hammer-dressed archcs)—(gauged arches corresponding with the ashlaring) to form their soffits outside wood frames; the soffits of windows being { 9 or / $4\frac{1}{2}$ } inches deep; and proper skew-backs being formed in all cases. All such arches to be close set and pointed.

No. 55. Reveals. All reveals of the said openings to be (trimmed to a neat face)—(also of brick)—(neatly dressed as arches)—(wrought to a neat sharp arris, as soffits).

No. 56. Rough arches. Turn rough arches and counter-arches wherever practicable, through the thickness of walls, excepting where they may not show in the external facing; and construct 12-inch rough relieving arches over all lintels, or bressummers, as sketch.

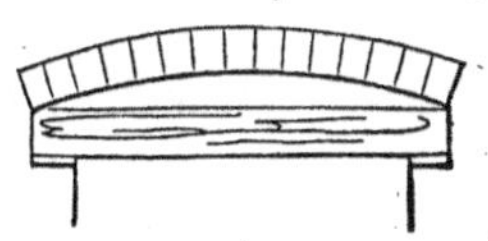

No. 57 Inverted arches, &c. (See No. 15.)

No. 58. To face, &c. (See No. 16.)

No. 59. Rough projections. Properly form all rough projections, corbellings, &c., for plaster string courses, fascias, pilasters, cornices, &c. Or, see No. 17, altering the word "brick" for . . . . .

No. 60. Fire openings and flues. Properly form all fire openings, with brick arches over the same; and brick trimmer arches where required for front hearths. Carefully gather in the chimney throat, and carry up flues round

Chimney stacks. cylinders of not less than 14 inches diameter in the clear, wel. pargetted. The chimney stacks above roof to be carried up in brick to the heights shown in drawing; and properly fix the chimney pots hereafter described. (See No. 19.)

No. 61. Rough coping. The walls of . . . . to be finished with a top course of large rough stones, partially hammer-dressed to a circular top edge; bedded on their *flat* edge, and well flush pointed with Aberthaw mortar.

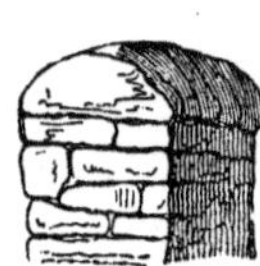

No. 62. Rough coping and cement. The walls of . . . . . to be finished with a top course of stone on edge, well bedded and jointed; to overhang the faces of wall 2 inches, and (when the masonry shall have perfectly settled) to cover the said coping with Roman cement, as adjoining sketch.

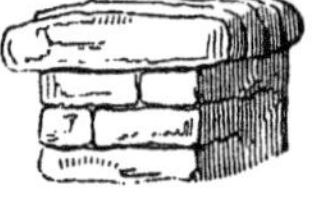

No. 63. To bed, &c., fix grates, &c. (See No. 21.)

No. 64. Build dwarf walls, &c. (See No. 22.)

No. 65. Bricknog. (See No. 23.)

No. 66. Vaults. (See No. 27 or 28, and 30 to 32.)

No. 67. Extra rubble-work. (See No. 34.) Party-walls. (See No. 35.)

No. 68. Cess-pits, drainage, dung-pit, dry area, and tank. (See Nos. 36 to 47.) Ventilation. (See No. 48.) Jobbing.. (See No. 49.)

No. 68½. Brick fittings. (See No. 49½.)

No. 69. Footing of paving stone. Provide and lay beneath the footings of . . . two complete courses of (Yorkshire) stone, of the several widths shown on drawings. The stones to be 3″ thick, each averaging 10 ft., and none less than 6 ft. superficial.

No. 70. Rough stone-work in masonry or brick-work.

Provide and fix—(here mention and describe the form and size of any *rough* or *roughly wrought* stone-work which has to be worked into the brick-work or masonry,—such as corbels for overhanging chimney breasts, or other masonry; for girders, or other timbers; rough lintels for windows or doors where flat arches are not practicable, and which are to be plastered; rough lintels over intercolumns; rough plinths to receive iron or wood columns and story-posts; rough templates to receive iron beams; &c). (In short, all stone-work that is to be hereafter concealed.)

No. 71. Wrought stone-work built into masonry, &c., or brick-work.

Provide and fix—(here mention and describe the form and size of any *wrought-fair* stone-work which has to be worked into the solid brick-work or masonry at the time of its building,—such as hinge-stones, lintels, solid plinths, bases, corbels, &c., which are unconnected with any other stone-work, uncovered by plaster, and used in plain buildings, which, in all other respects, are of common brick-work or rubble masonry). (Example.—The hinge-stones and lintel of a strong closet rebated for iron doors; the plinths under the piers of a shop front; &c.) (In short, all stone-work which does not partake of the nature of ashlar; which cannot, like stone steps or window-sills, be worked in after the masonry or brick-work has been carried up; and without the previous fixing of which the common walling cannot in any degree proceed.)

o. [illegible] Door steps, common.

To put to the . . . doors of . . . . , as shown on plan, plain solid tooled steps of {granite / Purbeck} stone, 12″ × 8″, properly back-jointed, and mortised for door-posts. Also a piece of paving of the same, to extend from step to outside face of plinth.

No. 73. Common stair flights.

To put from the . . . . to the . . . . . a flight of solid {granite / Purbeck} steps, 12″ × 8″, properly tooled (and holed for iron balusters), back-jointed, and securely (bedded on masonry / brick-work or (pinned into walls). (If there are landings describe them.)

No. 74. Better stair flights. To put from the . . . to the . . . a flight of solid Purbeck / Portland steps, wrought and rubbed smooth on all faces and soffits; back-jointed as sketch, the treads holed for balusters, and the steps securely pinned into walls. Landings of the same, inches thick, rebated on to last riser (and, if required, to have joggled joints run with lead).

No. 75. Stairs of paving stone. To put from the . . . to the . . . a flight of risers, treads, and landings, of inch tooled . . . . . stone (securely pinned into walls), or (bedded on brick-work or masonry). The treads mortised for balusters.

No. 76. Out-door steps, &c., better quality. To put to the doors of . . solid wrought and rubbed Portland stone steps (qy. with moulded nosings). Each step, out of

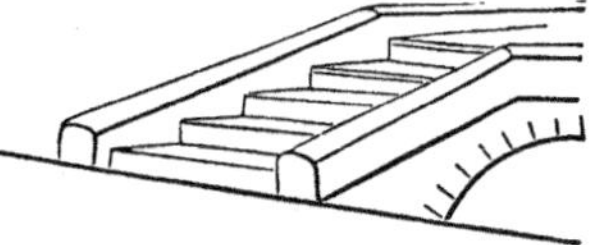

a stone inches by inches, properly jointed and bedded on the substructure (and flanked with Portland curbs, inches by inches, wrought, with rounded top, rubbed, and properly mortised for balusters). (If landing, state it.)

No. 77. Stone stairs, superior. To put from the . . . . to the . . . . flights of the best and hardest [marble, or] Portland stone steps, with moulded nosings, returned at ends, the soffits (as well as the rest) wrought and rubbed fair, bead flush-jointed, as sketch, and tailed full 9 inches into walls; the bottom step having its section a solid square, and finished with handsome curtail. The landings thereof to be full inches thick, with edge moulding to correspond with nosings of steps; the mid-landings being in one slab each, and the upper landing of . . . stones, tailed inches into walls, and joggle-jointed with lead. Each step and landing mortised for balusters.

No. 78. Stone stairs, handsome. To put from the . . . . to the . . . . flights of the best and hardest [granite, freestone marble, or] Portland stone steps, with moulded nosings along the front, outer end, and also along the back of each step ; the soffit

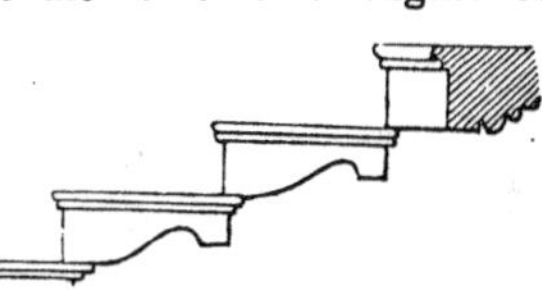

of each step (except those at bottom and landings) to be moulded as shown by sectional profile, and the whole tailed 9 inches into walls. Landings inches thick, having their soffits moulded and panelled as drawings, and their edges moulded to correspond with the nosings of steps. Handsome curtail to bottom step, whose section will be a solid square. The whole lapped and jointed as drawings. The mid-landings to be in one slab each, and the upper landing in . . . . stones, tailed inches into walls, and joggle-jointed with lead. All required holes for balusters.

No. 79. Stone steps and iron risers. To put from . . . . . to . . . . . a flight of Portland / Purbeck / Yorkshire } stone treads, with (rounded) (or moulded) nosings ; the risers thereof to be of open cast iron-work (see Smith), &c., &c.

No. 80. Window-sills, common. To put to the windows of . . . . . good common sills of . . . . stone, inches by inches; sunk, weathered, and throated, and 4 inches longer than the width of openings.

No. 81. Window-sills, superior. To put to windows of . . . . finely wrought (and rubbed) sills of . . . . stone, inches by inches (qy. moulded as drawings ?), and sunk, weathered and throated. The sills to be 4 inches longer than the (width of openings) (or than the united width of openings and jamb dressings). (Qy. whether corbels under the sills, &c. ?)

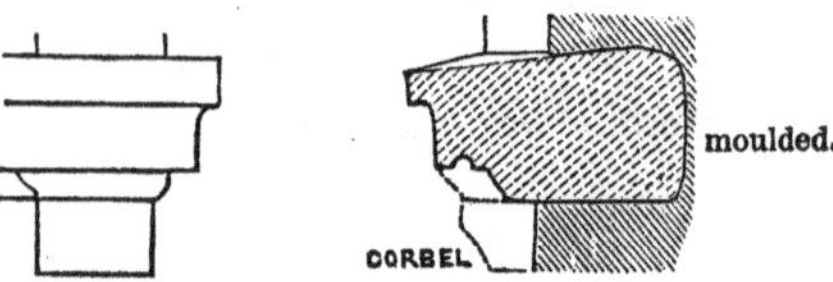

No. 82. Window-sills, common Gothic.

To put to windows of . . . . common sills of {(slate, Yorkshire stone, or Purbeck / (blue-stone, or red sand-stone} paving) stone, inches wide, 2½ or 3 inches thick, wrought-fair edge and ends, and laid sloping.

(The above will do, either for Italian or Gothic.)

No. 83. Window-sills, Gothic.

To put to windows of . . . . . sills of . . . . . stone, properly wrought throated, if projecting) (specify if in one or more heights, and make the *top* sill of one length, if possible).

Note, if two sills may be cut out of one stone, as sketch.

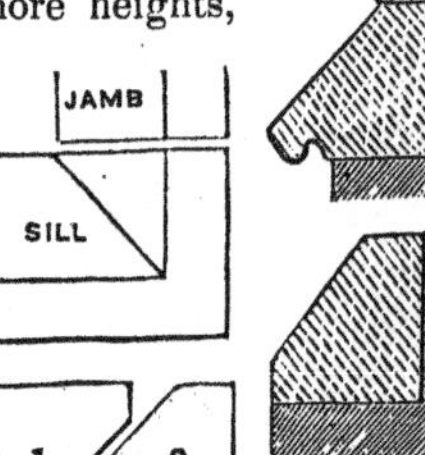

No. 84. Architraves to doors, Grecian or Italian.

To put to the doorway of . . . . . an architrave of the best solid . . . . . stone, moulded, and of the scantling shown by fig. drawing No. . The lintel to be of one stone; the jambs of {one / three / or more} stones down to plinth. The whole to be rebated, as drawings. (State if any of the jamb stones are to bond into the walls.)

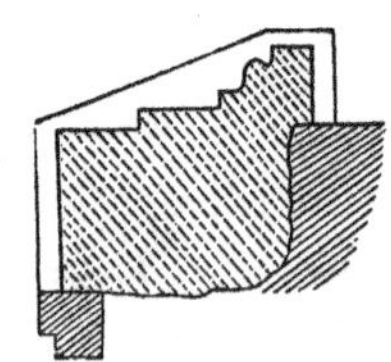

No. 85. Door architrave, and entablature.

To put to the doorway of . . . . an architrave, &c. (See No. 84.) Put over the architrave a frieze of similar stone quality in . . . . piece(s), not less than inches thick, of the height shown in drawing; and, above the frieze, a cornice of the sectional scantling and moulded profile also shown (and in . . . . . stone) (s).

No. 86. Door architrave, entablature, and pediment.

To put to the doorway of . . . . (all that is mentioned in Nos. 84 and 85) a pediment of the same stone and quality, the tympanum of one (or three) stone(s) not less than inches thick, and the raking cornices to correspond with that below, having the additional moulding shown on drawing.

No. 87. Door dressings, various and handsome.

To put to the doorway of . . . .
pilasters, architraves, &c., &c., &c.,

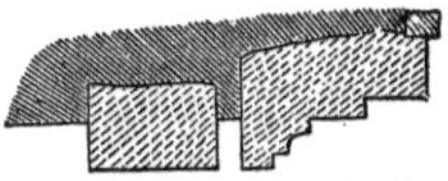

or

engaged columns, architraves, &c.,

or

pilaster dressings, as drawings,

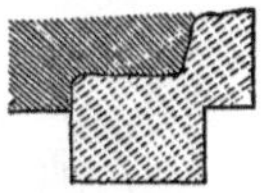

or

columns and jambs, as drawings, 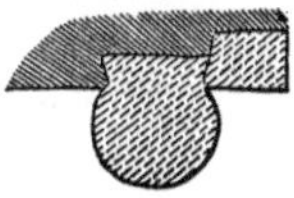
with
moulded bases, and capitals,
or with
Ionic, Corinthian, or enriched capitals,
or with
consoles plain or enriched, as drawings:
the pilasters, engaged columns, &c., to be of the best solid . . . . stone, in . . . . piece(s) (exclusive of caps and bases) and of the sectional form and scantling shown on drawings. The architraves, &c. (see Nos. 84 and 85), and, if pediments are required (see No. 86).

No 87½. If any other parts of the building are to be enriched, this may be reserved till the end as a general clause.

The capitals (and, if there be such, the enrichments, of architraves, friezes, cornices, consoles, &c.) to be executed in the very best style, after models of the full size, provided at the cost of the Contractor, and only adopted under the expressed satisfaction of the Architect.

No. 88. Window dressings, various. To put to the window openings of the . . . . . architraves, &c. (See No. 84, substituting the word "sill," or "blocking course," or "string course," for plinth) (or as the case may be).

No. 89. To put to the windows of . . . . . (See No. 85.)

No. 90. To put to the windows . . . . . (See No. 86.) (State whether the pediments are to be angular or circular, or whether they are to be both, alternating.)

No. 91. To put to the windows of . . . . . (See No. 87, and 87½.)

No. 92. Archivolts, &c. To put to doorway of . . . . . or the windows of . . . . . an archivolt, or archivolts of . . . . . the best solid stone, moulded, and of the scantling shown in drawing No. , with joints only, as shown on the elevation thereof by blue lines. (If a key-stone, describe it.) Imposts, &c., &c., &c. The imposts to said archivolt of similar material and quality, and of the substance and profile shown in drawings. (Qy. forming caps to pilasters or jambs? which pilasters or jambs will extend in . . . . . piece(s) to base, plinth, sill, string or blocking course, and be of the sectional substance shown on plan.)

No. 93. Gothic door dressings. To put to doorway of . . . . . a plinth, jambs, and archivolts of solid . . . . . stone, wrought, moulded, and of the sectional form and scantling shown by fig. , drawing No. .

No. 93½. The jambs to be of . . . . . stone(s) alternately bonding into walls; the archivolts of . . . . stone(s); and the same to be of . . . . . stone(s) in their recessed depth, as indicated in sections. (If there be imposts, caps, bases, plain-moulded or carved, other enrichments, and label or drip-stones, state them.)

No. 94. Gothic Tudor door dressings. To put to doorway of . . . . . a plinth and jambs of solid stone, with square head and spandrils inclosing an archivolt, wrought, moulded, &c., and of the sectional forms and scantling shown by fig. , drawing No. . (See No. 93½, and add thereto a description of the spandrils.)

No. 95. Gothic window dressings. To put to window openings of . . . . . jambs and archivolts of solid . . . . . . stone. (See Nos. 93. and 93½.)

No. 96. Gothic windows, superior. To put to window openings of . . . jambs and archivolts of solid . . . stone (see Nos. 93 and 93½), and properly cut, carve and fix the (columns, mullions, transomes, mullion arches (plain or foliated), spandrils, and the tracery complete), as shown on drawings. The (columns, mullions, &c.), to be of the sectional form and scantling shown in details, and to have joints only where marked by blue line on elevation.

No. 97. Gothic Tudor windows. To put to window openings of . . . jambs and square head of solid . . . stone (qy. inclosing mullions, transomes, mullion arches (plain or foliated), spandrils, and tracery) complete, as shown on elevation, fig. . The jambs, heads (mullions, &c.), to have the sectional form and scantling shown in details, and to have joints only where marked. Properly cut and fix also the labels or drip-stones.

No. 98. *Note.* Bay or Oriel; Italian or Gothic. Bay or Oriel windows, Italian or Gothic, will partake of the same *general description* as already given, to which it will be necessary to add a description of the plinth (under the sill), the angular piers or jambs, the blocking course, balustrading, &c. (if Italian): or the cornice and battlemented or pierced parapet (if Gothic). It may be also, that the Gothic oriel may rest on a moulded corbel (which must be accurately described as to con-

Balconies. struction); and that the Italian windows may have balconies before them (continuous, or attached separately), in which case they must be described, as formed of . . . . stone landing, inches thick (how wrought and moulded ?), tailed inches into wall; supported by carved brackets or consoles (as drawings) securely pinned inches into wall; and supporting a blocking course, with pedestals, balusters, capping, &c., wrought moulded, &c., as drawings.

No. 99. Plinth. To put along the . . . . a plinth of . . . . stone (neatly wrought) (wrought fine) (how tooled ?) (qy. rubbed ?), feet inches high, in {one / two / or more} stone(s) inches thick. The top chamfered, and no stone to be less than feet inches long. (See No. 109.)

No. 100. String course. To put along the . . . . a {wrought moulded / plain wrought} chamfered and throated (say what stone ?) string course, of the sectional form and scantling shown in detail. No stone to be less than feet in length. (See No. 110.)

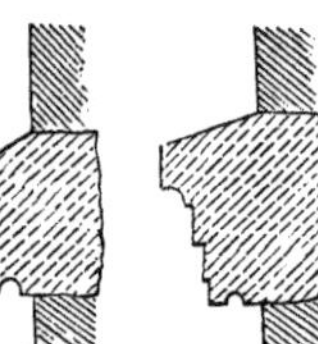

No. 101. Cornice. To put along the . . . . a cornice of . . . . stone (qy. in {two / or more} layers), of the sectional form and scantling shown in details, and no stone to be less than feet in length. (Enrichments to certain mouldings ? Modillions, plain or enriched ? (See No. 111.) Soffits sunk panelled, &c. ? Dentils ? Antefixæ ?) All the said enriched parts to be carved in the best style out of the solid, after models of the full size, provided at the cost of the Contractor, and only adopted under the expressed satisfaction of the Architect. (See No. 87½.) The plain parts wrought in the best manner, (qy.) {and rubbed ? / or tooled.}

No. 102. **Blocking course.** To fix above the cornice, all along the . . a blocking course of . . . stone,

or

Parapet. a parapet having a plinth, dado, and capping,

or

Balustrade. a balustrade course, composed of plinth, pedestals, balusters, and capping, as drawing; the same (or the several parts of the same) to be solid, and of the sectional form and scantling shown in detailed drawings. The plinth and capping to be in stones of not less than feet long. The balusters { square / turned / or otherwise } and half-balusters to pedestals. The whole to be (wrought fair) (tooled?) (rubbed?) (See No. 112.)

No. 103. **Chimney stacks.** The chimney stacks of . . . to be capped with . . . stone, moulded, and of the sectional form and scantling shown in drawing. (Qy. whether the shafts shall be also of stone entire; or stone ashlar.) (See No. 113.)

No. 104. **Quoin stones.** The . . . angles of . . . . to be finished with (roughly wrought) or (wrought, part rough, part tooled) or (wrought fair) and chamfer-channelled quoins of solid . . . . . stone, of the heights, lengths, and sectional form shown and figured on detailed drawings, two quoins being cut out of one stone thus: (See No. 114.)

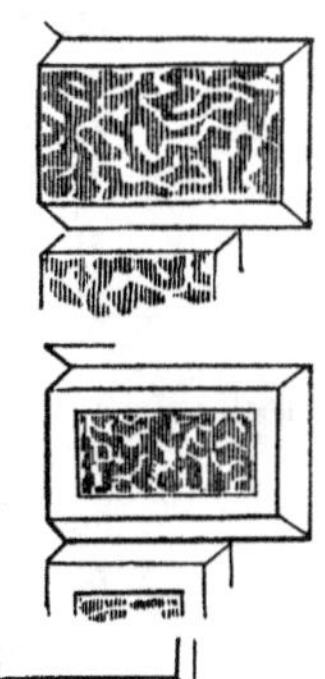

No. 105. Rusticated doors and windows, and arcades.

The { jambs / reveals / sills } and { heads / soffits / archivolts } of the (arches) (doors) or (windows) of . . to be formed of rustic-work of solid stone, corresponding, in material and workmanship, with the rustic quoins of main building; and of the form, size, and scantling, shown on detailed drawings.

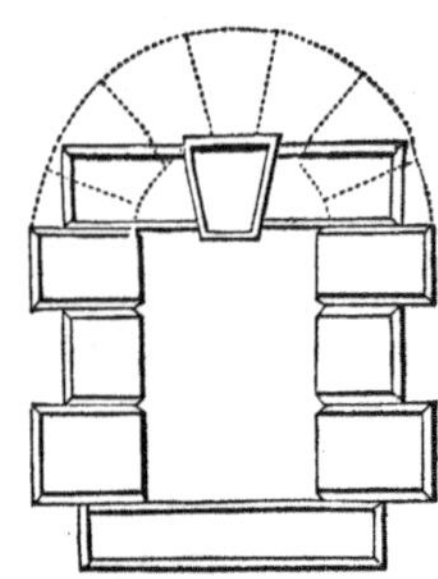

No. 106. Ashlaring, common and superior.

To face with . . . . stone ashlaring (roughly wrought) (wrought neat and tooled) (wrought fair and rubbed) and (square- or chamfer-) channelled, as shown by elevation, the whole of the . . . . . . properly forming the radiating channels of { flat / segment / circular } arches, and returning the channelling under soffits and against jambs or reveals of doors, windows (recesses? and all round (qy. insulated) piers.) (See No. 108.)

Or

No. 107. Ashlaring, the best.

To face with . . . . stone ashlaring, wrought fair (qy rubbed?) and worked close joint, the whole of the . . . (If there be no *architraves*, mention the radiating joints of { flat / segment / circular } arches, &c.) shown by elevation(s.) (See Nos. 108 and 115.)

No. 108. Ashlaring, how fixed, &c., &c.

The said ashlaring to consist, as nearly as circumstances will admit, of courses ′ ″ high; formed with headers, having a horizontal bed of ′ ″ by ′ ″; and stretchers, having a horizontal bed of ′ ″ by ′ ″; the quoin stones being in no direction less than ″ on their bed. All horizontal

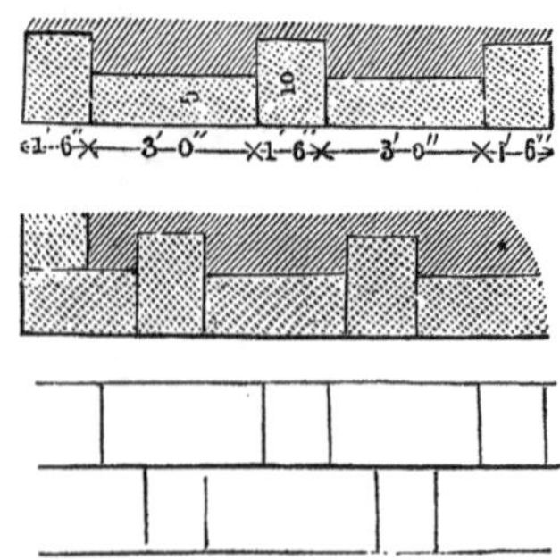

joints to have a slight chamfer on the upper edge of each stone. (See No. 115.)

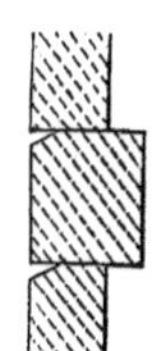

No. 109. Gothic plinth. Gothic basement or plinth. For general description, see No. 99. Add description of moulding and sub-plinth (if required), ", the same to be of the sectional form, &c., shown in details.

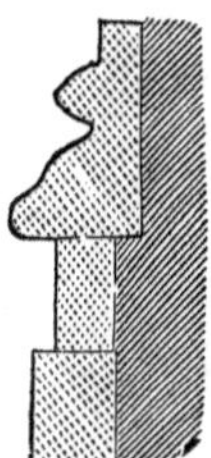

No. 110. String course, Gothic. Gothic string course. Same description as No. 100.

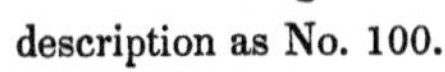

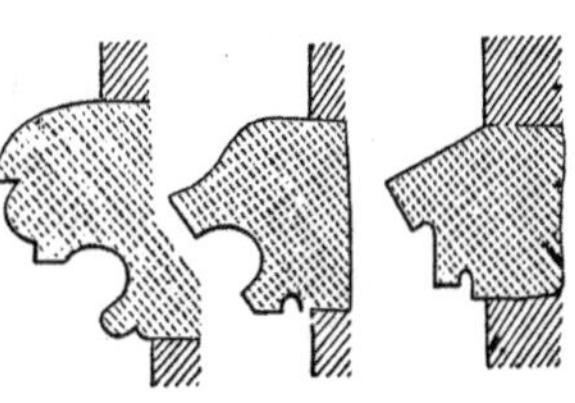

No. 111. Cornice, Gothic. Gothic cornice. Same general description as No. 101. Specify whether plain? with separate, or continuous enrichments?

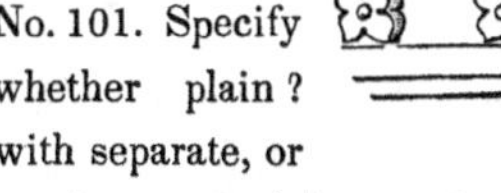

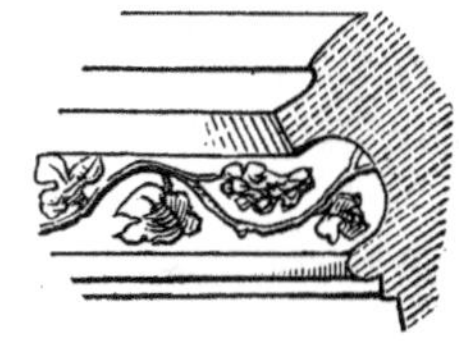

No. 112. Parapet, Gothic. Gothic parapet. To fix above the cornice (or string course) all along the . . . . . a (plain capped) or (embattled and

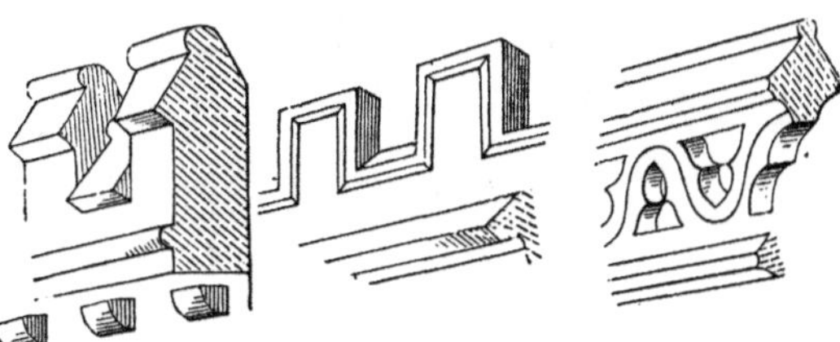

capped) or (embattled and moulded) or (open worked and capped) parapet of . . . stone, as drawings. The several parts of the same to be of the sectional form and scantling shown by details (the capping, if continuous, in stones of not less than ′ ″ long) (the open or sunk ornamental work carved in the best manner), and the work, generally, to be jointed as shown by blue lines on detailed drawing.

No. 113. Chimneys, Gothic. Chimney stacks, with (shafts) caps, bases, plinths, &c. (plain moulded) (embattled) (panelled) (or otherwise decorated) as drawings; the same to be of . . . stone, of the sectional form and scantling shown by details.

(Qy. whether the *plain* parts of the plinths, and shafts, may not be of brick; *the moulded work only* being of stone?)

No. 114. Gothic quoins. Gothic quoins. Same general description as No. 104. Ditto to doors, windows, &c. (See No. 105.)

No. 115. Gothic ashlar. Gothic ashlaring. Same general description as Nos. 107 and 108.

Buttresses. Describe buttresses. Whether formed with ashlar (as 1)? or

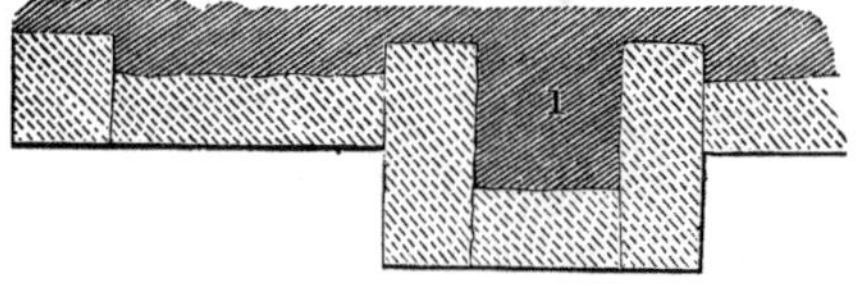

with solid work (as 2)? or part solid and part ashlar? or with heading and stretching quoins (as 3)? Whether wrought at

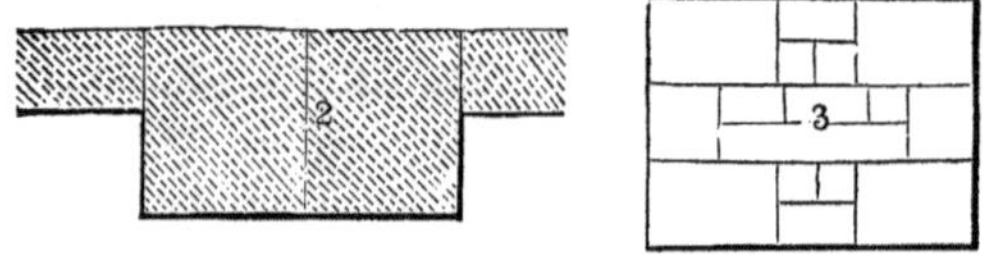

angles? panelled on face? or otherwise decorated?

No. 116. Buttress cappings.

The set-off, or several sets-off, of buttresses, to be capped with (plain or moulded) water-tables (of one or more stones), as drawings. The same to be of the same material and quality as . . . and of the sectional profile and scantling shown in details.

Or

No. 117. Gablet capping.

(same general description as No. 116, substituting for "water-tables," gablets (plain moulded) (topped with finials) (with carved finials and crockets), &c.

No. 118. Pinnacles, &c.

Or

(same general description as No. 116), substituting for "water-tables" gablets as described in No. 117) (and adding),

The top gablet to be crowned with (plain moulded) (moulded crocketed) (panelled) pinnacles, having carved finials, &c.

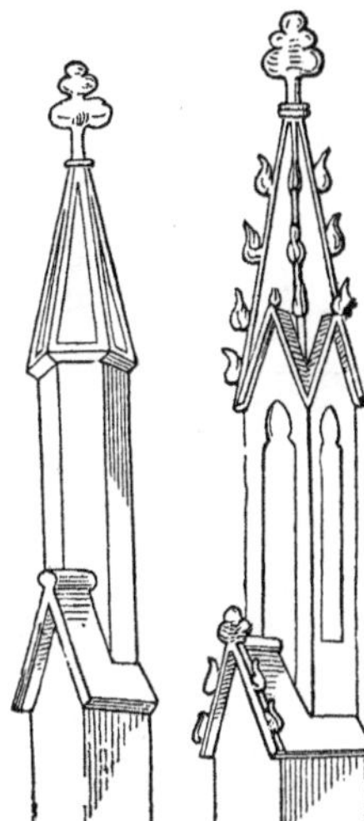

No. 1 9. Pediment, Greek.

The ashlaring in the tympanum of pediment to be precisely accordant, in the height of its courses, and construction, with

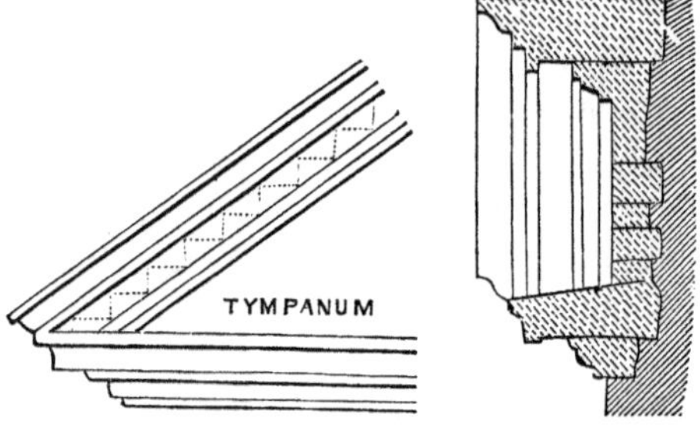

that of the (walls below, or general face of building). The horizontal cornice to be a continuation of (main cornice), omitting the top moulding; and the upper layer thereof to be of single stones from front to back, securely tailed into the masonry not less than inches, and no stone having a front length of less than ' ''. The raking cornices to be of the same form and scantling as that of (main cornice). The apex or meeting mouldings at top to be out of one block, having a horizontal bed on tympanum; and the raking cornice at the lower angles of pediment to be out of the same undivided block with the end of horizontal cornice. The hidden part of raking cornices to be cut in the form of steps, so as to have a series of horizontal beds upon the back masonry. The top stones of raking cornices

either thus, or thus,

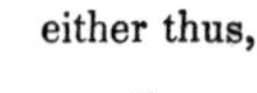

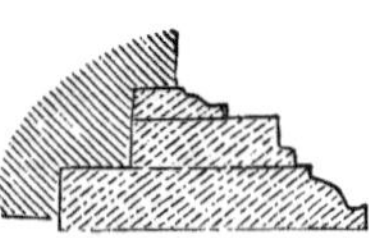

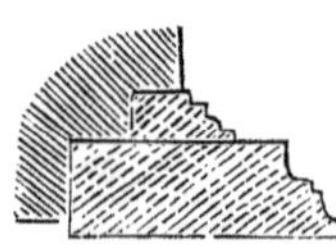

to be of one piece transversely; and no stone having a front length of less than ' ''.

If blocks, pedestals, or acroteria, describe them.

No. 120. Gables, Gothic. The gables of . . . . . to be capped with a (plain) (moulded) coping of . . . . stone, of the sectional form

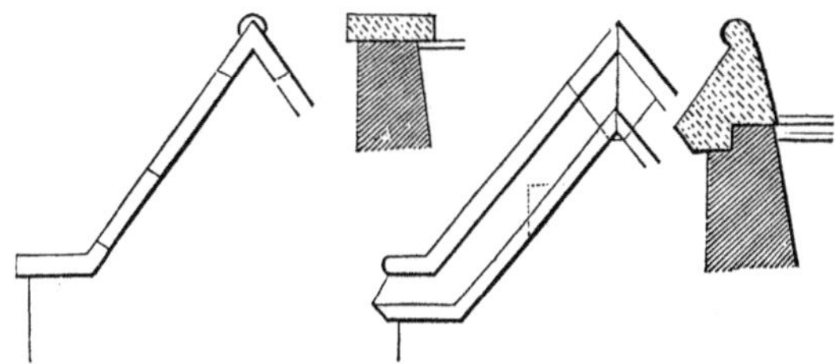

and scantling shown by detailed drawings, in lengths of not less than ′ ″ (back-notched for horizontal beddings), and with springing stones and apex-saddle stones cut of the solid, as also shown.

No. 121. Gothic gable corbels. (The springing stones to be supported by cut flush corbels, of the face and profile shown by drawings;)

or

(The springing stones to have a return face, supported by corbels of the face and profile shown by drawings) (the said corbels to be of *stone, serving to stop the eaves cornice or gutter*).

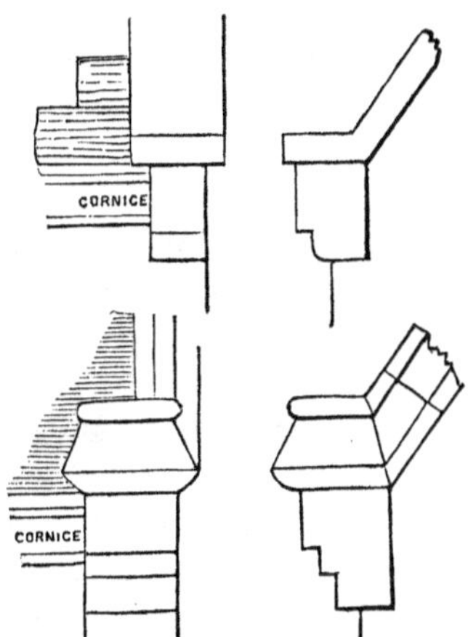

Portico. See Note, p. 96.

Portico, Greek or Italian.

No. 122. Plinth, cased. The plinth under the columns of the portico to be formed of top and side casing of . . . . stone, of the sectional form and scantling, and vertical jointing, shown in drawings, properly bedded on the (brick, or rubble) basement and core. The sub-plinth bonded into said core, having its bonding stones under the axes of columns;

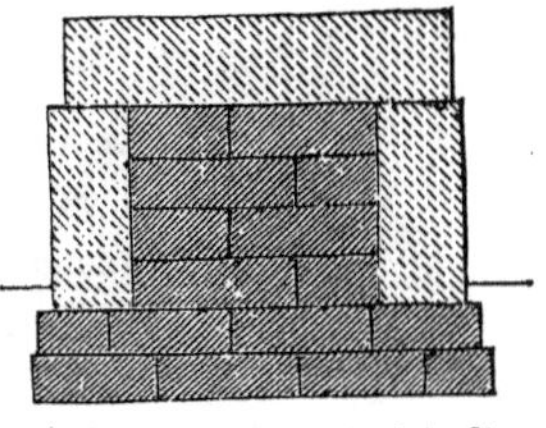

or

No. 123. Plinth solid. The plinth under the columns of portico to be formed solid, of . . . . stone, of the sectional form and scantling, and vertical jointing, shown on drawings;

and

No. 124. Back Plinth. A plinth, of ashlaring, to match the stone-work under columns, to be carried round the inside recess, or back of portico, as drawing.

No. 125. Columns, &c. The columns (antæ) and pilasters to be of . . . . stone, with (moulded, or moulded and enriched) bases and capitals, and (plain, or fluted) shafts, as detailed on drawings. The shafts to be in (one stone, or three stones), and the pilasters properly bonded into the main walling.

Note.

Portico. The portico will either be constructed with a substructure of common rubble, or brick; a plinth of brick, or rubble covered with cement;* columns of brick covered with cement; an entablatûre, &c., of rubble or brick (with rougn stone lintels over columns), also cemented;

or

the visible portions will be *partly* stone, as

1st. Stone plinth only;

2d. Stone plinth and columns;

3d. Stone plinth, columns, and architrave;

or

the visible portions will be *wholly* stone, with backings and fillings of rubble or brick, as the locality may require.

* [It is so very difficult to make cement stand in a northern climate, on any part of a substructure,—foundation, or basemen wall ***next the surface*** of the ground, that we recommend its omission in those parts ***below*** the water-table which are exposed to the weather. Let such wall be laid up in smooth courses, and pointed neatly and colored to correspond with the cemented exterior of the building above the water-table.]—*Ed.*

t will therefore be necessary,

under the heads of "Bricklayer,"

or "Rubble Mason and Bricklayer,"

to describe the foundations, and the *core* of the work; whether there are to be flat *stone footings, inverted arches* under the columns, *wood bonds and cores* to the brick columns, *relieving arches* over the same, &c., &c.*

Arcade. The same remarks will also apply to arcades. Such portions, therefore, as are not to be stone, will be described under the heads of "Bricklayer," or "Rubble Mason and Bricklayer."

No. 126. Architrave. The architrave to be of . . . stone (solid[1]) (or solid[2] up the first, or first two[3] faces) (or solid up to the crown[4] moulding) (*describe the casing to the part* NOT *solid*), of the sectional form and size shown by details, and *vertically* (or otherwise) jointed, as marked on elevations, or shown or described on detailed drawings. If enriched, describe it.

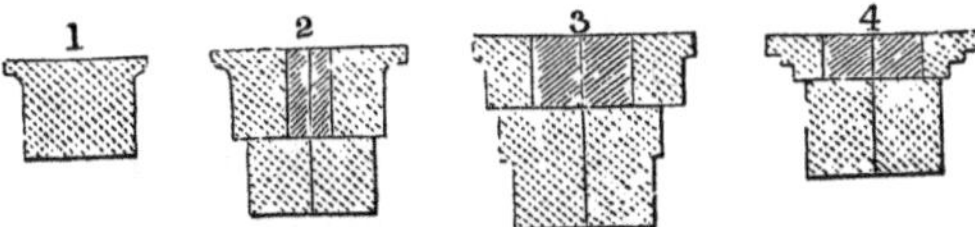

Note.—It is impossible to make any general description sufficiently accurate for this important member of a colonnade. A reference to a full detailed drawing, showing the stones separately, the mode of uniting them by arched or vertical joggled joints, the copper chain tie and hanging bar, and the relieving arches of the concealed brick-work or masonry, is the only way of insuring a clear understanding.†

No. 127. Return or back architrave. An architrave of ashlaring, to match that over the columns, to be carried (round and) along the inside (or back) *recess* of portico, as drawing. Qy. enriched?

* See Bartholomew's Specifications, No 4600.

† See Bartholomew's Specifications, No. 4610

No. 128. Beams in ceiling. If there be any inner longitudinal and transverse beams to form the ceiling of portico, they must be carefully studied, and here described. Qy. enriched?

No 129 Store soffit. If there be a stone ceiling altogether, here describe it. Qy. enriched?

No. 130. Frieze. The frieze to be formed of . . . . stone ashlaring, in no case less than inches thick, jointed as drawings; and the quoins to be cut out of solid stone, so as to show a return of not less than ' ". Qy. enriched?

No. 131. Cornice. To put along the front and returns of portico a cornice of . . . . stone. (See No. 101.) Qy. enriched?

No. 132. Blocking, parapet, balustrade. If the portico, instead of the pediment, &c., is to have a plain blocking course—or parapet with capping and plinth—or open balustrade (see No. 102). Qy. enriched.

No. 133. Pediment. Adopt the general description given at No. 119. If the portico be surmounted by blocks, pedestals, or acroteria, describe them. Qy. enriched?

No. 134. Various. Complete the description of the portico by explicit references to its landing, pavement, steps, guard-stones to preserve the plinth from carriage-wheels, &c.

No. 135. Arcades, Roman. Describe the plinths; whether solid or not. The piers; whether solid, or of ashlar; whether plain, or rusticated (see No. 104); whether there be plain or moulded imposts. The arches; whether with archivolts, or radiating stones, plain, or rusticated as piers; whether key-stones, plain or carved, &c.

No. 136. Arcades, Gothic. Describe the plinths; whether solid or not. The pillars (their bases, capitals, if any) and the number of stones to compose the shafts; the number of stones in the archivolts; and the quality of the work filling up the spandrils.

No. 137. Plugs, cramps, and lead. *Note.*—At the conclusion of the wrought ornamental cut stone-work insert a full description of the manner in which it is to be secured together by plugs of marble, stone, or copper; copper cramps; and lead plugging, and running; bearing also in mind the channelling and lead running of water joints on the upper surfaces of cornices, &c.; the safe application of chain bars; the provision of sheet lead in the joints, and under caps and bases of columns, as well as between any other stones which, without lead, may have their meeting arrises crushed by vertical pressure.

Enrichments. Casing. Final perfection. Particularly specify also the required accuracy, sharpness, &c., in the cutting of all enrichment, and the prior provision of satisfactory models (see No. 87½); and expressly state that the work shall be cased over, and finally left perfect and clean at the conclusion of the whole.

MISCELLANEOUS STONE-WORK.

No. 138. Coping. Cover the . . . . with . . . stone coping, of the sectional form and scantling shown by annexed sketch, throated under (one or both) edge(s) (qy. cramped with copper ?) and plugged at the joints with lead. (Qy. chased to receive flushing ?) (Qy. tooled, or rubbed ?) No stone less than ′ ″ long.

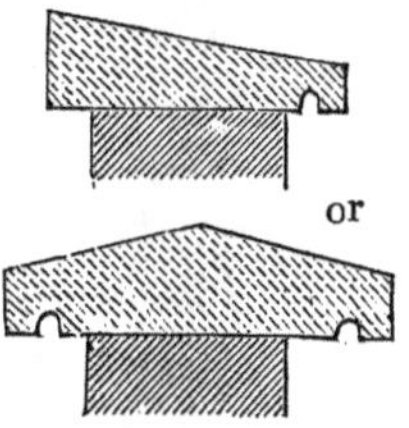

No. 139. Curbs. Put round the . . . a curb of . . . stone, of the sectional form and scantling shown by annexed sketch (qy. how wrought ?) (qy. cramped ?), plugged at joints with lead (and properly holed for iron railing). No stone less than ′ ″ in length. (See Plumber, No. 391.)

No. 140. Back hearths. Put to fire-places proper back hearts of . . . . . stone inches thick.

No. 141. Front ditto. Put to the fire-places of . . . . front slabs of qy. blue-stone ?—free-stone ? slate ?—Portland ?—marble ? (rubbed or polished, as the case may be) not less than inches thick; and inches longer than their respective fire-openings. The same to be inches wide.

No. 142. Chimney-pieces. Provide and fix to the fire opening of . . . . . a (slate) chimney-piece, valued at £ ; to that of . . . . a Portland ditto, value £ ; and to that of . . . . a marble ditto, value £ ; the Proprietor being at liberty to purchase all, or any of these, himself; the Contractor keeping distinct the allowance he has made for carriage and fixing.

No. 143. Paving, common. Pave the . . . . . with {Yorkshire / Purbeck / slate / limestone / blue-stone} paving, not less than inches thick, and no stone less than feet superficial; the same to be well bedded on a good bottom (of dry rubbish) and jointed in mortar.

No. 144. Better paving. Pave the . . . . with {Yorkshire / Purbeck / limestone / slate} paving (rubbed or tooled) surface; and rubbed joints not less than inches thick, and no stone less than feet square; well bedded on a well-rammed bottom, and close jointed in {mortar. / cement.}

No. 145. Superior paving. Pave the . . . . with Portland stone, inches thick, surface and joints rubbed fine; laid (square ? or diagonally ?) in stones not less than ' " square (or, as shown on drawings), with cement under the joints, on a course of brick-flat, as

sketch; the bricks being well flush-bedded in dry and well-rammed rubbish. (Qy. if any *marble* introduced with the stone ?)

No. 146. Marble paving. Lay the . . . . with a paving, formed of the different marbles, and of the size and pattern shown and described on drawing; the whole to be executed with the finest possible joint, and geometrical exactness, and to be left thoroughly and uniformly polished. (N.B. If the marble be valuable, state the minimum thickness it may have as a *veneer* upon Yorkshire or slate stone.) The paving to be not less than inches thick, and the joints laid in cement, on courses of brick-flat, firmly flush-bedded in dry well-rammed rubbish.

No. 147. Mosaic paving. Lay the . . . . with the mosaic paving of Wyatt, Parker, & Co., allowing the sum of £ for the same.

No. 148. Stone fittings to cellar. Form wine-bins in cellar with { slate / Yorkshire / &c. } slabs, inches thick, on half-brick piers, as sketch, having neatly wrought edge, each slab the full length and depth of bin; and provide and fix also neatly wrought shelves of similar stone in the larder and dairy, cutting water channel, as described on drawing.

Larder. Dairy.

No. 149. Trough. Put in the scullery a neatly cut trough of . . . . . stone, having a clear hollow of by and inches deep, with hole for waste water-pipe.

No. 150. A bath. Put in the . . . . . a bath, formed of slabs of slate, grooved into each other, and bolted with iron, as sketch, and of the clear internal dimensions thereon shown; the same to be internally lined with white glazed tiles bedded in cement; the top edges capped with (mahogany or marble) capping, and the exterior painted in imitation of white-veined marble. Form all necessary holes for supply and waste-pipes.

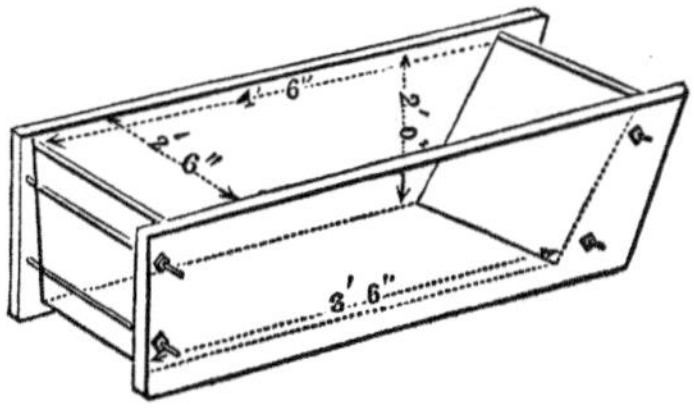

No. 151. Stone sills, heads, jambs, or hinge stones, to strong closet. State any other stone or marble fittings; as slabs in halls, or passages; washing basins of marble, &c.

No. 152. STABLES, Miscellaneous Stone-work in—

Sills and Steps.—Plinths to stall-posts, 8 inches square at top, 12 inches at base, neatly wrought 6 inches out of the ground, and 12 inches buried. Open surface gutter along front of stalls out of stone (8″ × 6″), and in lengths of not less than feet.

Sink-stones and gratings over drains.

Pavement. Pitch pebble-paving in sand.

Do. of dressed refuse stone, no stone less than 8″ × 6″ × 6″, close bedded in sand.

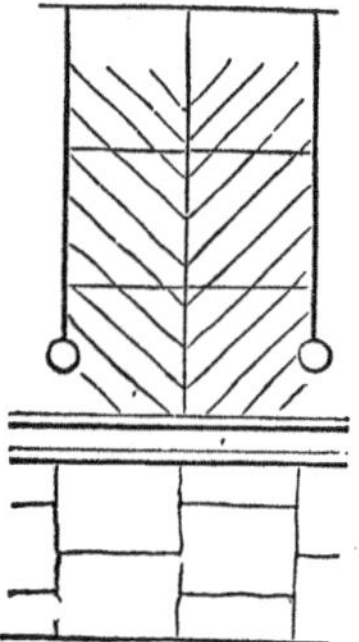

Do. of flat . . . . . . paving, no stone less than . . . . Those in stalls channelled to carry off wet; the rest rough tooled, and the whole well bedded and jointed on mortar.

Corn chest in loft, of slate or . . . . slabs, grooved into and bolted to one another, including a bottom ′ ″ by ′ ″, and sides and ends feet high.—A . . . . . . chimney piece in saddle-room. (Qy. saddle-room paved ?)

No. 153. COACH-HOUSES, Miscellaneous Stone-work in—

Plinths of . . . . . stone to the coach door or story-posts, or piers, of the size and form shown and figured in sketch.

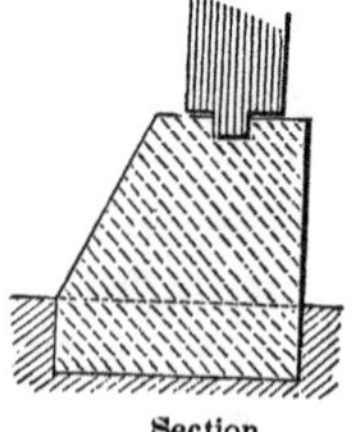

Section.

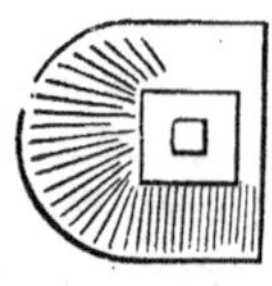

Plan.

(If stone piers: state whether *wholly of wrought stone?*—in *one?* or how *many* stones? or whether *hinge stones only* are required, to be built into brick-work or rubble?)

Stone to receive bolts of meeting doors.

Curb stone under doors from plinth to plinth. (Qy. whether *pebble-paved?* paved with *dressed refuse?* or *flat-paved?* Guard stones to keep the wheels of different carriages apart, and to stop them at back.) (If there be a story of masonry above the coach-house door openings, there will of course be *piers* instead of wood posts, and, instead of a wood bressummer, there will be lintels of stone, as *a, b, c, d, e,* jointed as drawings, and of the scantling

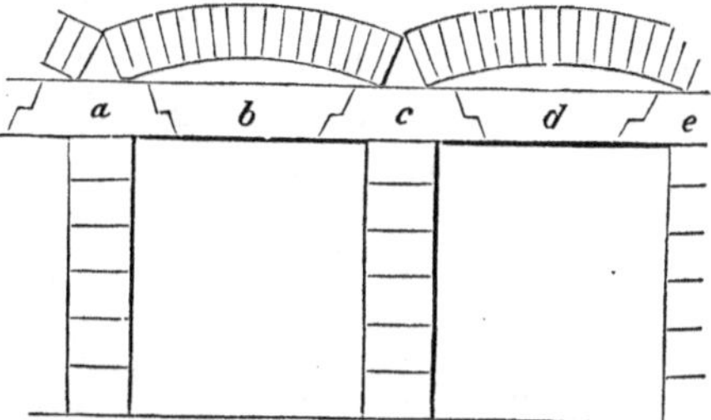

thereon figured; with *relieving arches* provided under the head of "Bricklayer" or "Rubble Mason.") Describe any rebating there may be in the stone-work, and how the wrought stone-work is to be finished on the face—cramps, plugs, lead running, &c. Steps, sills, &c. Also any corbels which may be built into walls to take the ends of girders.

No. 154. STABLE AND OTHER YARDS.

Pitch-paving in sand, properly laid to a current, with sinks and gratings.—Coping stones to dung-pit.—Coping to walls and boundary walls.—Stone caps to gate piers.—Gate piers, either partly, or wholly, of wrought stone. Stones for hinges, bolts, &c.—Plinths to posts of sheds.—Curbs from plinth to plinth, and under gates.—Stone drinking-troughs.—Curb and cover-stone to man-hole of tank.—Pebble or flat-paving to cow-houses, piggeries.—Feeding-troughs to ditto.—Plinths to posts, and open stone gutters, &c., to cow-house.—Coping to outer pig-sty &c., &c.—Hinge stones to pig-sty doors.—Curb stone under ditto.—Steps and sills to cow-houses, and other out-buildings having doors and windows.

No. 155.

SLATING.

No. 156. Slating, common.

Cover the roofs with good scantle slate, on sound heart of oak single laths, and oak pins; no slate to be less than   " by   " and the whole to be well plastered against the pin with lime and hair mortar. The lap of upper slates over the lower to be not less than 2 inches. Properly cut double rag hips and eaves, and cut heading course.

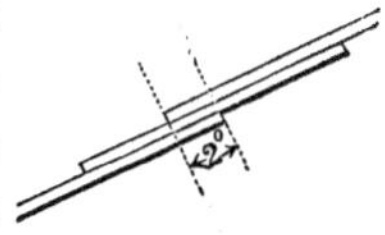

No. 157. Better slating.

Cover the roofs with { large / small } lady slates { 16" × 8" / 14" × 7" } nailed with cast iron nails (boiled in oil) to battens 2" × ½", and well plastered underneath with lime and hair mortar. The lap of upper over lowest slate to be not less than 2½ inches. Properly cut double rag valleys, hips, eaves, and heading course.

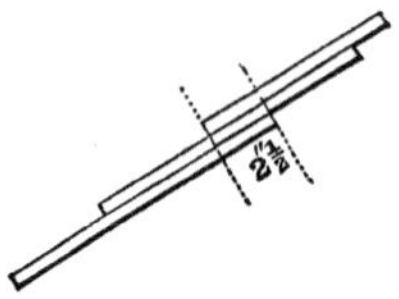

No. 158. Improved slating.

Cover the roofs with { countess, viscountess, or / large lady slates, }   " by   " nailed with cast iron nails (boiled in linseed oil) to battens 2" by ½", and pointed outside with putty of whiting, oil, and sand. The lap of upper over lowest slate to be not less than 3 inches. Properly cut hips, eaves, and heading course.

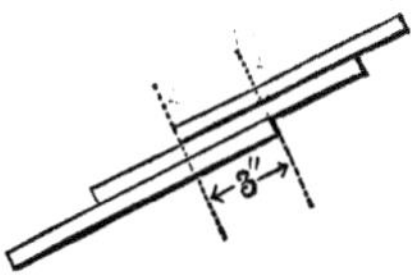

No. 159 Superior slating.

Cover the roofs with { queen / princess / rag / duchess / marchioness / countess / viscountess } slates,*   " ×   "

* Queen's, 3′ × 2′.

Princesses, 26 inches long, varying in width from 13 to 20 inches nailed with copper nails to battens ″ × ″. No slate to have less than a lap of { 4 / 3½ } inches over the lowest slate beneath it; and every slate to have at least two nails. Eaves, hips, and heading courses to be formed of cut slates, so that their bond may be uniform with all the rest. All the horizontal overlays to be well bedded (1½ inch up, from the edge) in (the stucco paint cement of Johns & Co., Coxside, Plymouth). The raking or vertical meeting edge joints to be laid on a bedding of the same cement 3 inches wide.

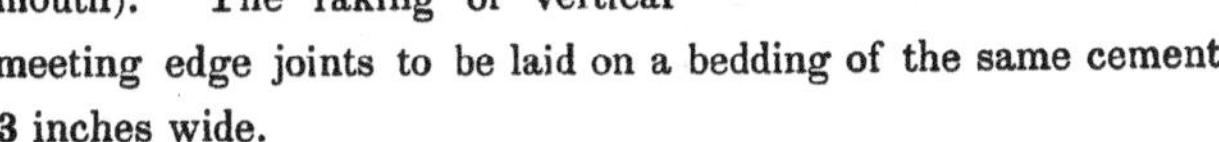

No. 166. If the skeleton roof be of iron, the last description will serve, substituting "strong copper wire" for hanging the slates, instead of "nails."

averaging not less than 16 inches wide, weighing about 5 tons 3 cwt. per 1200, and covering about 16 squares.

Ditto, 28 inches long, varying in width from 14 to 21 inches, averaging not less than 17 inches, weighing about 6 tons per 1200, and covering about 18 squares.

Ditto, 30 inches long, different widths, from 15 to 22 inches, averaging not less than 18 inches, weighing about 7 tons per 1200, and covering about 21 squares.

Rags of large size, 17 dozen weighing a ton, and covering 2¼ squares.

Duchesses, 24 by 12 inches, weighing about 3 tons 7 cwt. per 1200, and covering about 11 squares.

Marchionesses, 22 by 11 inches, weighing 2 tons 14 cwt. per 1200, and covering about 9 squares.

Countesses, 20 by 10 inches, weighing about 2 tons 3 cwt. per 1200, and covering about 7¾ squares.

Viscountesses, 18 by 9 inches, weighing about 1 ton 13 cwt. per 1200, and covering about 6 squares.

No. 161. If the roof be over a circular building, state that the slates are to be cut to radiating joints from apex to eaves.

No. 162. **Best slating for very flat-pitched roofs.** Cover the roof of . . . . with imperial slates not less than 2 feet 6 inches by 2 feet each, and full inch thick; uniformly laid, with their ends meeting in a close joint along the upper surface of each rafter; each superior course to lap over

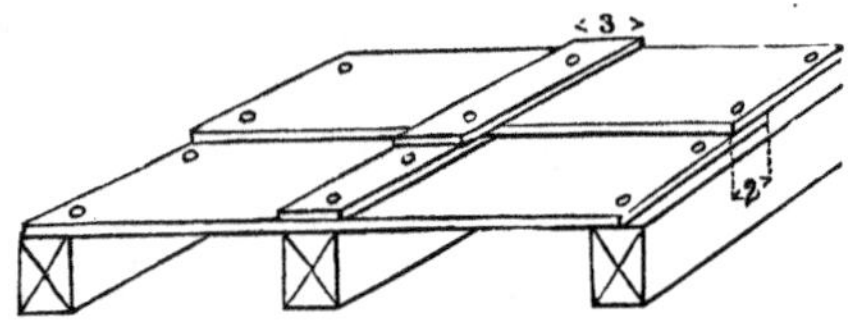

the course below at least 2 inches; and the vertical, or meeting joints, to be covered with imperial slate slips not less than 3 inches wide. The over-lap of slates, and the slate slips, to be well bedded in (the stucco paint cement of Johns and Co., Coxside, Plymouth). Each slate screwed to the rafters with two 1½″ screws, and two 2″ screws to each slip. All visible edges of the slates and the slips to be sawn or rubbed to a perfect smoothness; and make uniformly close the cement pointing at the finish of the whole.

No. 163. **Outside pointing.** Where the slates are not *laid* in cement, they may be externally pointed, after laying, as follows: The over-laps and meeting joints, throughout, to be made close with Johns' patent cement and sand, worked in with a stump brush, and the whole colored as slates.

No. 164. **Slate ridges, common.** Hips? (and) Ridges } to be covered with imperial slate slips, inches wide, inches thick, and in lengths of not less than ′ ″, securely screwed to rafters; close stopped at all meeting joints, and bedded on the slates 1½ inch up from the bottom edge with (Johns' patent paint) cement.

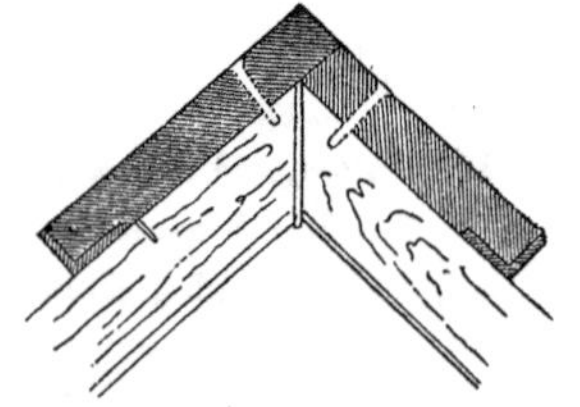

No. 165. Slate ridges, superior.

Hips ? (and) Ridges } covered with imperial slate sad- 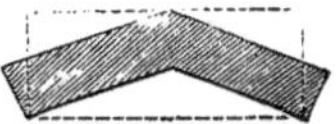 dle-cut capping, of the size and sectional form figured and shown in sketch, and in lengths of ′ ″; securcly screwed to rafters with screws, and jointed and laid in cement, same as the rest of the slating.

No. 166. Filleting.

Fillet the slating, wherever requisite, against the { brick-work / masonry } with (Johns' patent paint cement, mixed with equal parts of sand).

No. 167. Queen slating, of various sizes.

Cover the roofs with . . . . . . The slates to be inches wide. Their length to commence (say 36 inches) long, at the gutters, and to diminish gradually to (say 30 inches) at the ridges ; the same *bond* being observed throughout.

No. 168. Final clause.

Examine, and perfectly make good, the whole of the slating, at the close of the works.

TILING.

No. 169. Tiling, plain.

Cover the roofs with good plain tiles on double heart laths, laid to a proper gauge in { cement, / lime and hair / mortar, } each plain tile secured by an oaken peg.

No. 170. Ridge and hip tiles.

The ridges (and hips ?) to be covered with proper ridge (and hip ?) tiles, secured by T nails dipped in pitch, and hip-hooks also pitched, and set in { cement, / lime and hair mortar.

No. 171 Pantiling.

Cover the . . . . . with the best sound pantiling, laid to a proper gauge, on pantile laths, and effectually pointed on the inside with lime and hair mortar. (*Note.*—If for the roof of a brewery, or other building, requiring ventilation, or escape for steam, &c., the pantile *laid dry* is excellent.) Ridges and hips, as No. 170.

No. 172. Final clause. The who.e of the tiling to be left perfect at the close of the works, and no mortar to show externally to the disfigurement of the surface.

PLASTER AND CEMENT-WORK.

No. 173. Johns & Co.'s patent paint cement, inside work. Cover the partitions and battened walls with one coat of the paint cement, mixed with very fine sharp and clean sand, on lath and first coat of common lime and hair plaster. Cover the rubble walls with the said paint cement, on a render of common plaster, as aforesaid. Cover the brick walls with simply one coat of the said cement. The cement to be worked to a { fair or fine } surface, with a { wood or steel } float; and the whole to be carefully applied according to the printed instructions of the Patentees.

No. 174. Keene's cement. Keene's cement may supersede wooden angle beads, &c., &c.

No. 175. Commonest internal plastering. Lath, lay, and set the ceilings and partitions of . . . . , and render, set, the walls of . . . . .

No. 176. Common 3-coat work for ceilings and papering. Lath, lay, float, and set the ceilings and partitions of . . . and the battening against walls; and render, float, and set the unbattened walls.

No. 177. 3-coat work for painting or color. Lath, lay, float, and rough stucco the partitions and battened walls; and render, float, and rough stucco the unbattened walls of . . . . . (Qy. whether jointed to imitate ashlar ?)

No. 178. Best 3-coat work for paint or paper, &c. Lath, lay, float, and finish with trowelled stucco, the partitions and battened walls; and render, float, and finish with trowelled stucco, the unbattened walls of the . . . . (Qy. if jointed ?)

No. 179 To whiten all the ceilings.

No. 180. Color the walls and partitions of . . . a . . . color.

No. 181. Run all beads, quirks, &c., to angles of arched soffits, and where else required.

To properly plaster all sides, backs, soffits, &c., of window or other recesses, arches, ceilings under stairs, and other parts not cased with joinery, so that they may finish in conformity with the adjoining plastering.

No. 182. Cornices and enrichments. Run, all round the ceilings of the various rooms, the cornices, and execute the various enrichments, as shown and described on the drawing of "Plasterer's Details," sheet No. . Models of all enrichments to be first made (qy. at the expense of the Contractor ?), and casts therefrom finally approved by, and deposited with, the Architect, before the enriched work be commenced.

No. 183. Cement skirting. Run round the floors of . . . . . a skirting of (Keene's patent ?—Roman ? Johns and Co.'s ?) cement, of the size and sectional form shown by annexed figure.

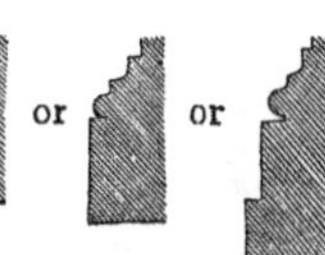

No. 184. Scagliola, &c. Execute, in the best Scagliola composition, the shafts of the columns, pilasters, &c., in the . . . . ; the Scagliolist engaging to provide the wood firring and cradling necessary to receive his work. The shafts to be in imitation of { verde antique ; sienna ; jasper ; } the caps and bases to be executed in Keene's patent cement (qy. whether the entablature, or any part of it, is to be Scagliola or Keene's cement ?), and the whole brought to the utmost polish, and left perfect.

No. 185. Johns & Co.'s patent cement, outside brickwork. Cover the whole of the external surface of the brick walls with one coat of the patent stucco paint cement, mixed with sharp clean sand, and applied according to the printed instructions of the Patentees.

Or,

No. 186. Common, on rubble. Cover the whole of the external surface of the rubble walling with a render of common lime and hair, and one coat of the patent stucco, &c., &c. (See No. 185.)

Or,

No. 187 Superior, on rubble. Cover the whole of the external surface of the rubble walling with a first coat of the patent stucco paint cement, mixed with very coarse sand; and a second coat of ditto mixed with a finer sand. (Qy. jointed?)

No. 187½. Rough cast, on rubble. Cover the external walls of the . . . . . with a render and float of common lime and hair, slap-dashed with a rough-cast of fine clean washed gravel and lime water. (Colored?)

No. 188. 2 coats, common, and 1 Aberthaw, on rubble. Cover the external walls, where not otherwise covered, of the . . . . . . , with a render and float of common lime and hair, and a stucco of Aberthaw [Thomaston] lime and fine sharp clean sand. (Qy. jointed?) (Colored?)

No. 189. 1 coat, common, and 2 Aberthaw, on rubble. Cover the external walls, where not otherwise covered, of the . . . . . . , with a render of common lime and hair, a float of Aberthaw [Thomaston] lime, &c., and a stucco of Aberthaw, jointed to imitate ashlar.

No. 190. Aberthaw, on brick. Cover the external *brick* walls, where not otherwise covered, with a float of Aberthaw, &c., and a stucco of the same, jointed to imitate ashlar.

No. 191. Run, in properly prepared { Aberthaw lime cement, / London Roman cement, } all parts of the external work hereinafter described, viz.—

a. The moulded cappings and plinths of chimney spills.

b. The top front and inside (to flashing) of parapets.

c. The rail, balusters, and plinth of balustrade.

d. The entire cornice, including the top surface thereof.

e. The mouldings, enrichments, &c., &c., of the frieze and architrave.

f. The strings, edges of rustics, channels of rusticated parts.

g. The architraves of doors and windows of the . . . . . fronts, including the whole girth from the back of moulding at A, to the wood frame at B.

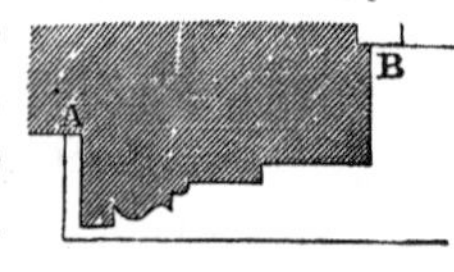

h. The moulded work of the entablatures, pediments, of doors and windows.

i. The cornices, trusses, &c., to doors and windows.

j. The pilasters, columns, bases, and capitals, of doors and windows.

k. The sills of windows.

l. The top of main plinth, or the plinth entirely.

m. The parapet and moulded work of portico, as cornice, architrave moulding, caps, bases, and (if fluted) shafts of columns, plinth, &c., and such other parts as are not to be executed in stone, or which cannot be as well finished in stucco.

The whole of the aforesaid Roman cement-work to be colored in imitation of the other plastering.

No. 192 All parapets, having lead flashings, to have a bed of cement right through them immediately above and touching the flashing.

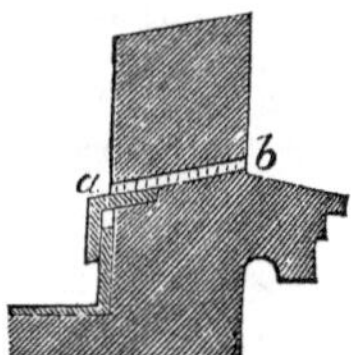

CARPENTERS' WORK.

No. 200. Carpenters' work, inclosures, &c.

Provide and fix all the timbers, boarding, &c., necessary to form the protective inclosures. (See No. 1.)

Construct also an office feet by feet clear, and feet high, to the springing of roof, for the Clerk of the Works (see No. 1), the same to be formed of weather-boarding on stout framing, having a properly hung and glazed window, also a door in frame, with strong hinges and good lock; a drawing desk feet long by feet deep, with drawer under; a stool; rail and pegs for cloak and hat; a corner cupboard with brass-knobbed latch. Floor properly boarded on joists.

No. 201. Shoring and old materials.

Provide and fix all required timber for shoring, &c. (See No. 2.)

No old timber to be used in the new works, unless permitted under the handwriting of the Architect.

No. 202. Piling and planking. Provide all the timber necessary for the piling and planking of the foundations, as described before. (See No. 10.)

No. 203. Sundries. Provide and fix all required scaffoldage, centering, turning pieces, beads, stops, fillets, tilting fillets, backings, blocks, cradlings, firrings, bearers, and all other minor articles of carpentry necessary to the perfect and efficient completion of the various works particularized under the heads of Carpenter, Joiner, Mason, Bricklayer, Slater, Plasterer, and Plumber.

No. 204. Bond, &c. Lintels. Provide all necessary wood-bricks and templates of sound old English oak, with every required preparation for fixing grounds, battens, and joinery; also the various courses of bond timber and wall plates, described, shown, and figured on the drawings; also lintels of old English oak over all square-headed window, door, or other openings, *within* the brick or stone arched soffits, it being clearly understood, with reference to *external* doors and windows, that no lintel shall appear *outside* the head of the wood frame. The said lintels to have a vertical depth of $1\frac{1}{4}$ inch for every foot of opening between the templates, and not to be longer than sufficient to cover the templates. One or more lintels, as required, to fill up for the thickness of the wall above; and the Carpenter to see that the relieving arches before described (see No. 56) are turned by the Mason. Templates to lintels not to exceed the scantling of 4″ × 3″.

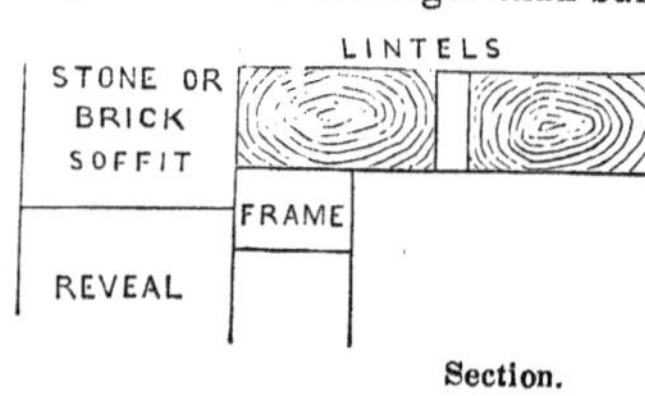

Section.

Elevation.

No. 205. Story-posts. Provide and fix the story-post (or posts) as shown in drawings; the same to be of the soundest Memel fir, and of the full figured scantlings, with cast iron boxed and tenoned caps and bases, as sketch, $\frac{3}{8}$ths thick.

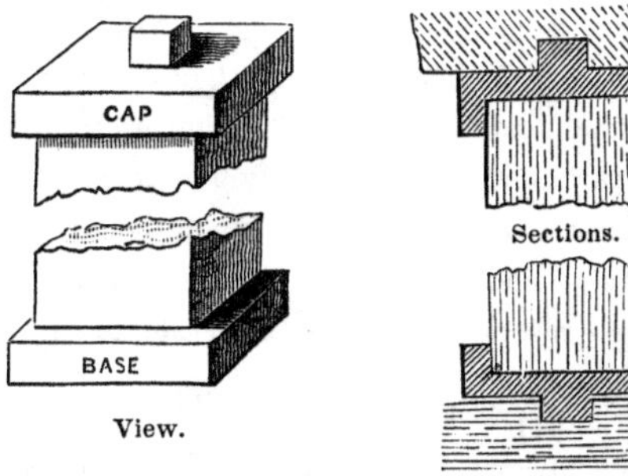

View.

Sections.

Stone base.

No 206. **Bressummers.** Bressummers of the soundest { white pine / Memel fir } to extend over (here describe, whether from pier to pier, or over story-posts, or iron columns, or otherwise, wherever they have to be constructed contemporaneously and for the support of masonry) . . . ; the same to be of the full figured scantlings, and formed of single timber, halved, reversed, trussed with wrought iron (king or queen) bolts, abutment ditto, struts, and straining piece, and bolted together with proper nuts, screws, &c., as shown by drawings. The whole screwed up to a camber, and mortised for the tenons of the story-posts (or iron columns), taking care to leave the mortise free for a lateral thrust in the event of the camber settling again to a perfect horizontal.

Elevation. Plan.

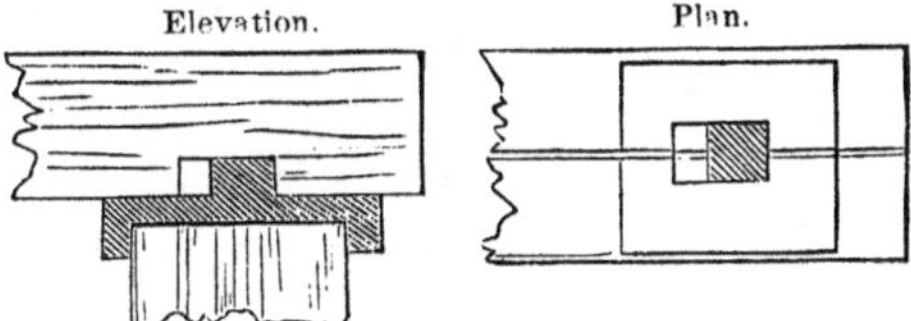

N.B.—It is possible the bearing between the supports may be so small as to require no iron trussing. The Architect will here use his own discretion; as the *weight above*, or the *flooring bearing on* the bressummer, *may* require his serious consideration.

No. 207. **Quarter partitions.** Sills of quarter partitions, resting on masonry, to be of sound old English oak, 4″ × 3″ (in very large buildings 6″ × 4″

See also No. 235. The scantlings for the *usual* partition are here stated. When the partition exceeds 12 feet high, an increased size should be given). Heads and braces 4″ × 3″. Principal quarters, as door-posts, king or queen-posts, straining pieces, &c., to be not less than 4″ × 4″. Common quarters 4″ × 2¼″, and 12 (16 or 18) inches from middle to middle (as the importance of the building, or of any particular part of it may require). No quarter to have a length of more than feet, without horizontal stiffening pieces, as *a*, *a*. The whole, except the sills resting on walls as aforesaid, to be of Memel fir / white pine on ground floors. (They *may* be, if economy require it, of sound American red pine on the upper floors.) All partitions hanging over voids to be truss-framed in the most careful manner with king or queen-posts, bolted with wrought iron to the sills or ties; struts and straining pieces to be properly framed into the same, and the whole rendered perfectly independent of the floor level with their sills.

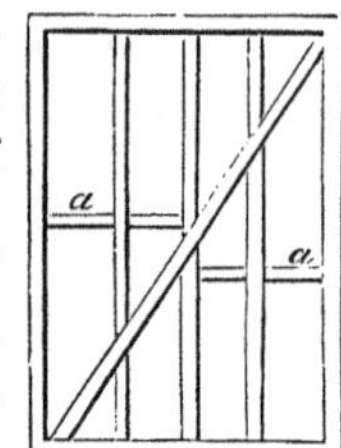

N.B.—In particular cases sketches or drawings of these trussed partitions should be made; and it will be sometimes advisable to have the king and queen quarters of *oak*.

All required quarter partitioning to form closets, &c.

No. 208. Ground joists. Ground joists to be of sound old English oak or Memel fir ″ × ″ and {12 / 14 / 1} inches apart, on oak plates 4″ × 3″.

No. 209. Common joisting. The rooms and passages, landings, &c., of (describing them with reference to the plans) . . . . . . to be laid with {hemlock / Memel fir / red pine / yellow fir} joists; those of (such and such rooms) ″ × ″, and inches mid to mid, &c., &c., &c. The whole to be properly framed into binders or trimmers, and to have a 6-inch hold in walls, bearing on plates 4″ × 3″. All trimmer joists to have an excess of 1 inch in thickness over the others.

No. 210. Binders and girders. Here describe any binders or girders that are to be employed in connexion with the common floor joists, as to landings in staircases, or over any other internal openings where the joists cannot rest on walls or partitions.

No. 211. Single-framed floors

The floors of . . . . . . to be formed of { white pine / Memel fir } binders ″ × ″, and not more than six feet apart, on oak templates 4″ × 4″, and having a hold of 9 inches on walls, with bridging joists thereon of { Memel fir / red pine } 6″ × 2″, and { 12 / 14 } inches apart, and ceiling joists thereunder $2\frac{1}{2}$″ × $1\frac{1}{2}$″, and 12 inches mid to mid.

No. 212. Double-framed floors.

The floors of . . . . . . to be formed of { white pine / Memel fir } girders ″ × ″, not more than 10 feet apart, on oak templates 6″ × 4″, having a hold of 12 inches on walls, with binders 8″ × 5″, not more than 6 feet apart, framed into girders, and resting on oak templates 4″ × 4″, with a 9-inch hold on walls. (Bridging and ceiling joists as No. 211.) If the girder exceed 20 feet long it must be trussed, as described for Bressummers, No. 206.

No. 213. Floor trusses, &c.

In churches, theatres, public rooms, &c., where there are galleries and floors rising in steps to different levels, accurate drawings must be given of the main trussed frame-work; and the specification will therefore especially refer to these drawings, as thus:

The rising floors of . . . . . to be supported on trussed frame-work, as drawings. The trusses (in such or such positions,—or not more than feet apart) of the full figured scantlings, put together in the most workmanlike manner, and with wrought iron bolts, straps, nuts, screws, &c., as drawings. The king or queen timbers of sound oak; the remaining timbers of { Memel fir; / red pine; } binders for floor and ceilings; bridging joists or firrings for different levels of floor, and ceiling joists; the whole as drawings. Breast-work to front of galleries truss-framed, as drawings, of material corresponding with the floor trusses, with iron bolts and straps as shown, and of the full scantling figured.

No. 214. Cross straining.

All (single-joist unframed) floors to have a range of cross bonding of fir pieces 2 inches square (as sketch),

closely butted and firmly nailed between the joists at parallel distances not exceeding 6 feet. (This will not be done in inferior buildings, nor where the joists are to be visible. See No. 228.)

No. 215. Ceiling battens. The joists of (such and such) floors to have ceiling battens 1½″ × ¾″, and 12 inches mid to mid, underneath them, to insure a good ceiling for the rooms below.

No. 216. Flats. Here introduce a description of the girders, binders, bridging and ceiling joists,—or of the binders, bridging and ceiling joists,—or of the simple joists only,—which may be required to support the lantern and lead flats of staircases, or the flats over porticoes, bay windows, or other parts of the building; either making explanatory sketches on the specification, or referring to detailed drawings whereon the scantlings are all figured.

No. 217. Lanterns. Here introduce a description of the rough carpentry necessary to raise the sill of the lanterns above the flats; also of the joisting or rafters necessary to form the flat or roof *over* the lantern. Scantlings as drawing.

No. 218. Roofs, Italian. The roof over the . . . . . to be supported by trusses, as shown and figured on drawing No. . These trusses to be not more than {6 to / 10} feet apart, with half trusses at the ends of corresponding form and scantling; hip rafters ″ by ″, properly framed into a dragon piece of oak ″ by ″, the said dragon piece dovetailed into an angle tie of {white pine, / Memel fir,} feet long and inches square. The tie-beams to have a hold of {18 / 12 / 9} inches on the walls, notched on oak templates, long and inches square. King or queen-posts of oak, with wrought iron straps or bolts (or both), to unite them with the tie-beam. Principals of {red pine / Memel fir} also united to tie-beam with wrought iron bolts, straps (or both), and the remaining timbers of roof, viz. the (assistant principals ?) struts (straining beams ?) (straining sills ?) ridge-piece, ridge-roll, purlins, pole-plate, and common rafters, to be likewise of { red pine; / Memel fir }; the whole framed in the most workmanlike manner, and the tie-beam to be wedged and bolted up to a camber of inches. Valley rafters ″ by ″.

Continue to describe the secondary and collar-beam, lean-to roofs, &c., in their turn. For curb roof, see No. 223. For projecting eaves, see No. 226.

No. 219. Roofs, Gothic. *Note.*—In these, it is likely there will be no tie-beam, nor any angle tie or dragon pieces. Collar-beams, hammer-beams, brackets, springing pieces, &c., will supersede the tie-beam. The valley rafters may remain; but there will be no half trusses at the ends. An accurate drawing of the roof must be made, the reference to it in the specification being only general. (See No. 222.) For curb roof, see No. 223.

No. 220. Dormer doors and windows. Provide, frame, and fix all the rough carpentry necessary to form the dormer doors and windows in the roofs, as shown on drawings.

No. 221. Boarding and battening for lead and slates. Lay the roof with { ¾ or / inch } rough Memel boarding for slates. Inch gutter boarding on proper bearers to parapets, and boarding for valley gutters, &c.; 2-inch drips. (See No. 222.)

Or,

Lay the roof with Memel fir battens 2″ × 1″, for slates. Inch gutter boarding, &c., &c., as before.

N.B.—If the roof have projecting eaves, there will be no parapet gutter boarding required.

Lay the several flats, roof of lantern, &c., with { ¾ or / inch } rough boarding for lead, forming proper rolls for joints and drips.

No. 222. Open or Gothic roof. It may so happen in the case of an *Italian* roof, and it will most likely occur in that of a *Gothic* roof, that the timbers are to be left visible from below; and that the specification must therefore describe whether they are to be "wrought fair," "cut," "moulded," or "decorated" as drawings. In a church, chapel, or Gothic hall, for instance, which has no plastered ceiling, "the roof," or "so much of it as is visible," would be so described; and the slates, or lead covering, instead of being laid on "rough boarding" (as in No. 221), would be laid on "inch deal boarding with (rebated and beaded) (or ploughed, tongued, and beaded) joints, and wrought fair underside."

No. 223. Curb roof. Curb roof over the . . . . . as drawings. Raking side, or sides, of { Memel, red pine, } formed by framed and braced quartering, as described for quarter partitions, No. 207: the tie-beams, king or queen-posts, principals, purlins, struts, rafters, &c., &c., together with the iron bolts or straps, necessary to the strength of the work, to be referred to "as shown on drawings," and the description of the Italian roof, No. 218, to be followed out as far as it is suitable; also the suitable particulars in Nos. 220 and 221.

No. 224. Garrets. Red pine binders from (tie-beam to tie-beam) or (collar to collar ″ × ″, and ceiling joists ″ × ″; not more than inches mid to mid. Fir ashlaring from the (raking quarters, or the rafters) to the floor joists, as section. Dormer doors and windows, as No. 220. Trap doors, No. 225.

No. 225. Ceiling floors. Red pine binders ″ × ″, and not more than feet apart, framed into tie-beams; and ceiling joists ″ × ″, not more than inches mid to mid. Chase-mortised into the binders. Openings for trapdoors into roof where marked on plans; and a rough boarded foot-way to be formed from the trap to the dormer doors, windows, or ventilators in roof.

No. 226. Projecting eaves. Provide and fix all rough carpentry necessary to form the projecting eaves, the finishings of which will be described under the head of Joiner.

No. 227. Troughs, cisterns, &c. Construct rough { white pine red deal } water-troughs for lead lining, to conduct from . . . . . through the roof to the cistern, or cisterns, at . . . . . . ; the said trough to be inches wide and inches deep in the clear. Construct also the cistern, or cisterns, of the sizes and in the situations figured and shown in drawings, fixing the same on proper bearers. Cover to cistern, if it be outside.

No. 228. Joists, wrought fair. *Note.*—In some cases, as in cottages, stables, &c., &c., the upper joists of floors and lofts will be brought fair with beaded angles ; also the girders, binders, &c. (See No. 260½.)

No. 229. Sound boarding. The spaces between the joists of the floors of . . . rooms to be fitted in with sound boarding on proper fillets ; and the Carpenter to see that the space between the said boarding and the floor boards be filled in with proper pugging [or deafening] of sufficient thickness.

No. 230. Sundry rough work. Provide and fix all required fir bearers and rough carpentry to the stair flights, &c., &c., &c.

Here go over the plans very carefully, from the roof through every floor downwards, and make as particular allusion as you can to the numerous minor features which may be peculiar to the design under consideration, and which cannot be considered in this general outline. Thus, in roofs and ceilings, ventilating apertures may be required. Sky-lights are to be prepared for, and quartering for rough boarded linings. Preparations may be required for hanging pictures ; for hanging lamps to ceilings ; for completing certain forms, which can only be done partially with real masonry ; for forming jambs, arches, inclosures, roofing to porticoes, porches, sheds, covered ways or projecting windows, &c., &c., &c.

No. 231. Battening. The internal surface of the several walls, marked by a yellow line on the plans, to be prepared for the Plasterer with { white pine / Memel deal } battens 2″ × 1″, and 12 inches mid to mid.

No. 232. Cradling and firring. Prepare for the arched, groined, or coved ceilings ; for the cornices, beam-work, panelled ditto ; for the entablatures, pilasters, and all other work that is to be finished by the Plasterer, with good and sufficient cradling and firring.

No. 233. Columns, &c., and lowered ceilings.

Provide and fix also all required rough carpentry to form the cores of Scagliola or wood columns, with whatever framing or trussed work may be necessary above them; and all binders and joists that may be required to such ceilings as are lowered beneath the floor joists above.

No. 234. Final clause.

The whole of the aforesaid Carpenter's work to be executed with sound and well-seasoned timber, free from sap, shakes, and injurious knots, and to be framed together with workmanlike skill and accuracy. The scantlings to be full, *after the saw;* and the iron bolts, straps, trusses, screws, nuts, &c., employed in the roofs, partitions, and bressummers, to be of the best iron, well hammered and wrought. The ends of all tie-beams, girders, binders, and other important bearing timbers, to be left free from mortar on all sides, so that the air may circulate around; and all joists, and the plates on which they rest, to have their concealed ends well coated with coal tar. Wherever the fir timber is not described as of Memel or Baltic, it will be taken up as American.

No. 235.

N.B.—In the event of sliding doors being desired between rooms, the quarter partitioning must be prepared accordingly with double framing, leaving the required space between.

JOINERS' WORK.

No 240. Ventilator to roof.

Here let the specification allude to any drawing there may be for ventilator, turret, or other piece of joinery rising on the roof.

No. 241. Sky-lights.

Prepare and fix sky-lights, as drawing, of 2½-inch Memel casement and bars in proper rebated and beaded frame, with all required means for rendering the same weather-tight.

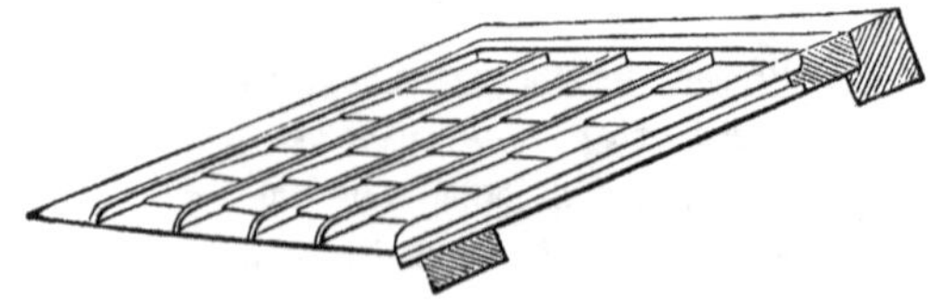

No. 242. Ceiling, or dome inner lights.

Plan.

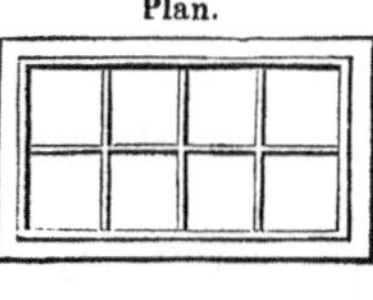

Prepare and fix a 2-inch { pine / red deal } neatly moulded light, in proper rebated and beaded frame, as sketch, in the ceiling floor under the sky-light (qy. whether it is to open ?), and inclose the space between the two lights with a neat deal boxing, leaving a door properly hung in one of the sides to allow of cleaning.

Section.

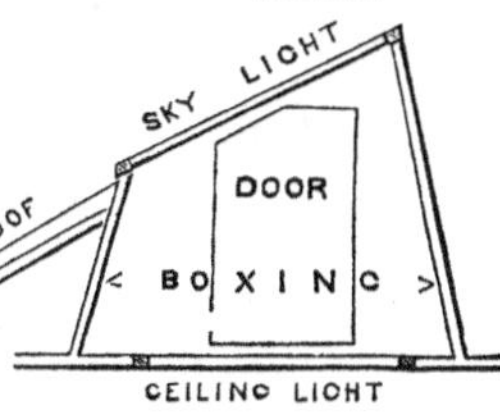

Or,

Prepare and fix a neat deal dome-light, in proper rebated and beaded frame, as sketch, in the ceiling floor, &c., &c., &c., as before.

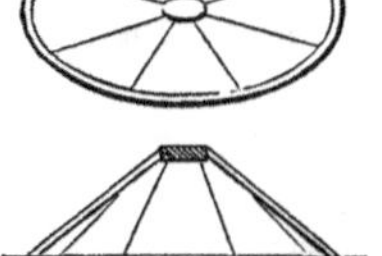

No. 243. Light and ventilation of water-closets.

It is well, when practicable, to light, and at the same time ventilate water-closets, by an adaptation of Nos. 241 and 242, lifting the sky-light on blocks so as to admit of air passing under the lower edge of the casement, and raising also the inner light for the same purpose. A dome-light would be best for a water-closet.

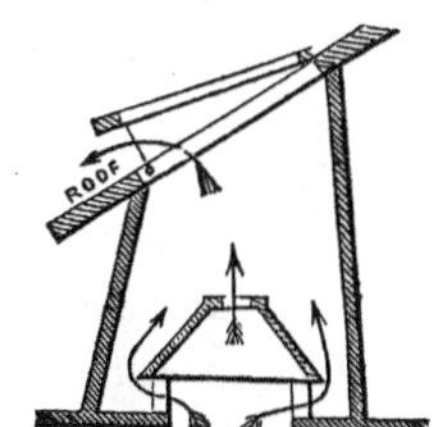

No. 244. Dormer door.

Provide and hang in proper heads and jambs 2-inch Memel deal bead-butt and square dormer doors, as shown on drawings, with hingeing and fastenings complete.

No 245. Dormer windows.

Fit up, with { 1½ or / 2-inch } Memel { casements, / or sashes, } in { solid re-bated / or deal-cased } frames having oak sills (qy. mullions ?) the dormer window openings, and fix window board ; the whole as drawings.

No. 246. Trap door. Frame and fix an $1\frac{1}{2}$inch bead flush and square trap door, in proper rebated frame, for ascent into the roof where shown on plans, with hinges and fastenings.

No. 247. Gutter cornice to eaves, Italian. Inch { white pine / Memel deal } gutter cornice to be fixed to the eaves of the . . . . . roof, having both a fixed and a falling bottom, with moulding on the front, as drawing, and of the dimensions there figured.

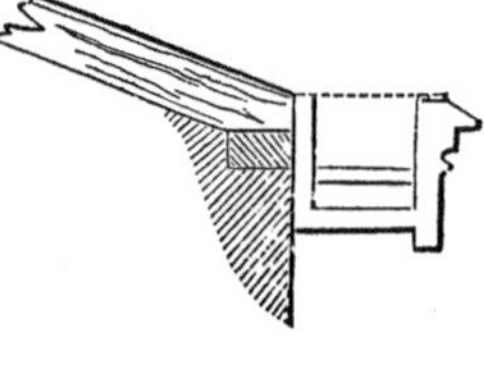

Or,

No. 248. Ditto, projecting. . . . . (same as before; adding) the same to project from the face of wall as shown, and to have a boarded soffit of inch deal, ploughed and tongued joints.

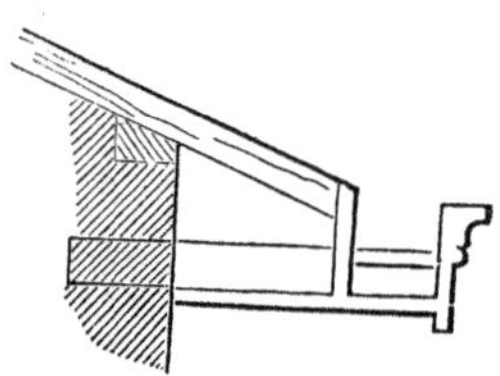

Or,

No. 249. Ditto, cantilever. . . . . . (same as Nos. 247 and 248; adding) also deal cantilevers, cut, moulded, and framed, at intervals of ′ ″ apart, into an inch Memel deal fascia board, having moulding to correspond.

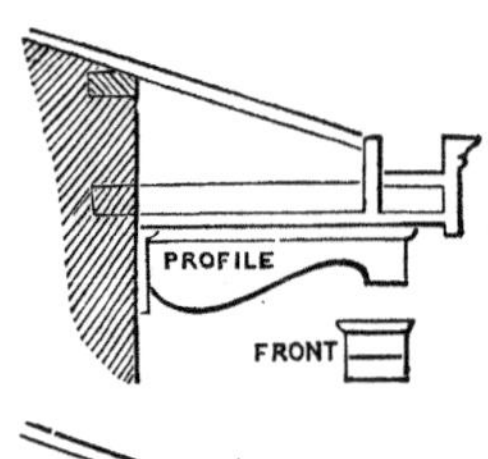

No. 250. Eaves, cornice, Roman. Cornice to eaves to be formed of Memel deal, framed, glued, blocked, and moulded as drawing, with cut modillions at intervals of inches apart; and a gutter, of the clear dimensions shown in section, and having a falling bottom, to be formed behind the upper mouldings of the cornice.

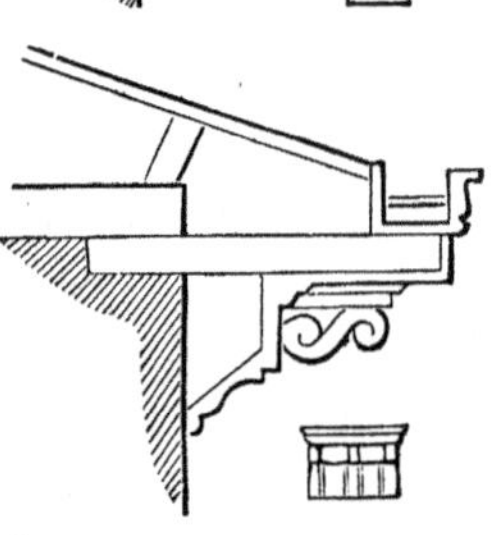

No. 251. Ditto, Gothic. Cornice to eaves to be formed of Memel deal, framed, glued, blocked, and moulded as drawing, with rain-water gutter, of the clear dimensions figured, and having a falling bottom formed in the upper part.

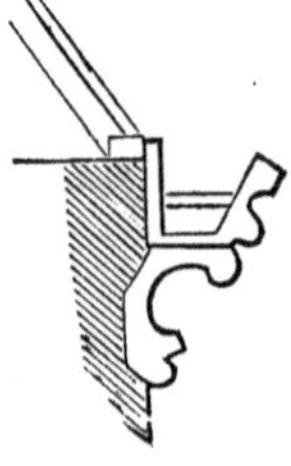

No. 252. Barge-boards. The raking eaves of gables to be fitted with inch Memel deal, moulded and beaded barge-boards, as drawing, to cover the ends of purlins.

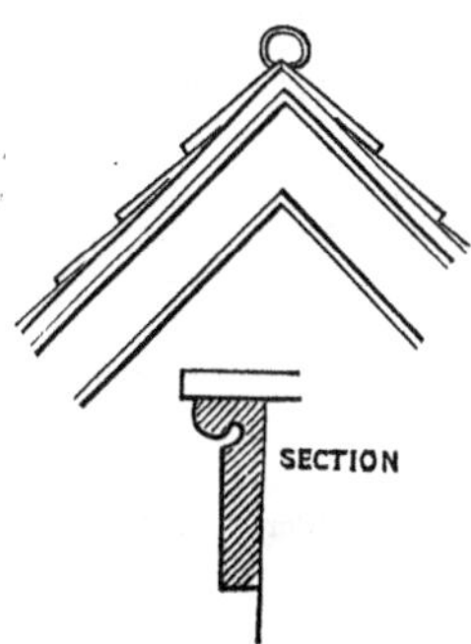

No. 253. Barge-boards, Gothic. The raking eaves of gables to be fitted with 2-inch { oak / pine } cut and moulded barge-boards, as drawing, the same to cover the ends of purlins.

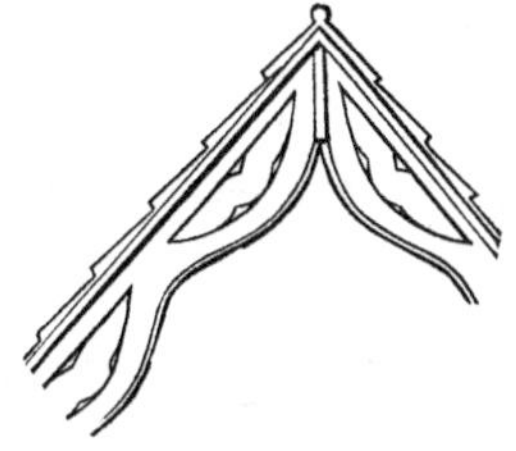

No. 254. Lanterns. Lantern-light over the . . . to be formed of 2-inch Memel deal casements, in solid { white pine / Memel fir } rebated and beaded frame, with oak sill rebated, double sunk, weathered and throated, and fascia with moulding all round the top, from under the lead, to 1¼ inch over the joint between the head-piece and the casement. The whole to be wrought and moulded as shown by the drawings. (See No. 290.) (Qy. if any of the lights are to hang.)

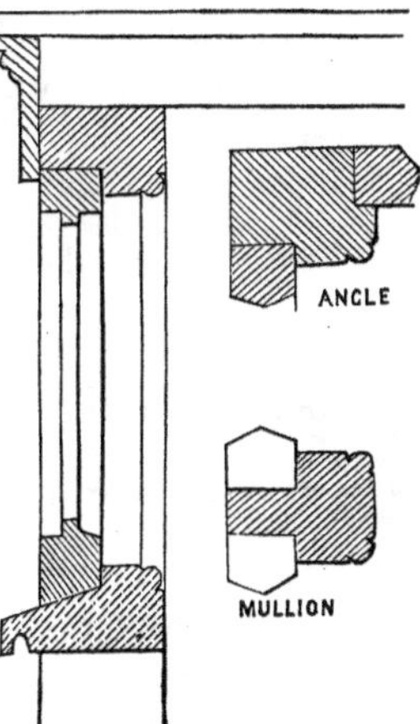

No. 255.

No. 256. Floors. Boarding common.

Lay the floors of . . . . . with inch . . . . deal folding; no board to exceed inches wide.

No. 257. Ditto, better.

Lay the floors of . . . . with { inch or 1¼-inch } deal, straight joint, face-nailed heading splayed; no board to exceed inches wide.

No. 258. Ditto, superior.

Lay the floors of . . . . with { inch or 1¼-inch } { wainscot, deal, oak, } straight joint, skew-nailed on one edge, and joints rebated:

or,

No. 259. Ditto.

—and joints ploughed and tongued:

or,

No. 260. Ditto, best.

—and joints dowelled with oak pins, at { 6 or 8 } inches apart:

(add to either of the foregoing three, viz. Nos. 258, 259, or 260) headings ploughed and tongued, and no board to exceed inches wide; neatly mitred margins to hearths, and the boarding grooved for skirting.

No. 260½.

State where floor boarding is to be wrought fair underside.

No. 261. Very superior floor of deal and wainscot, or of wainscot wholly.

Lay the floors of . . . . . with 1¼-inch { wainscot or Memel } best boarding, free from knots, and no board to exceed { 4 or 5 } inches wide, skew-nailed on one edge, dowelled with oak pins 6 inches apart; headings ploughed and tongued; and wainscot margin feet wide (measuring from the skirting, which will be grooved into the same), all around the rooms, accurately mitred at all angles, with grain running parallel to the ends and sides of the room respectively.

No. 262. Inlaid floors.

If the floors are to be laid in panellings and fancy patterns, an accurate drawing must be made and referred to.

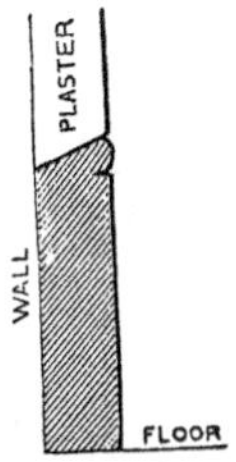

No. 263. Skirtings. The rooms and passages . . . . . to have ¾-inch deal beaded skirting, 4 inches high, and flush with plaster.

Or,

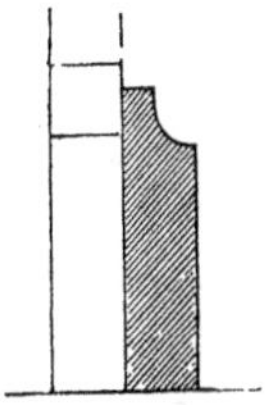

No. 264. Ditto. . . . . ¾-inch deal hollow-moulded skirtings, plugged to walls, 4 inches high.

Or,

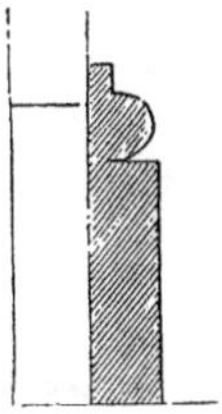

No. 265. Ditto. . . . . ¾-inch deal skirting, 6 inches high; fillet and torus moulded, and plugged to walls.

Or,

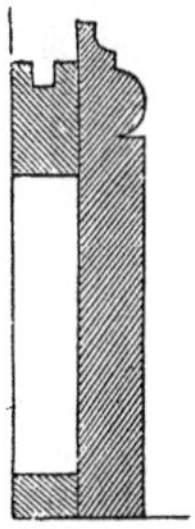

No. 266. Skirtings. . . . . ¾-inch deal skirting, with plinth 6 inches high, nailed to fillet and grooved grounds, and hollow and torus moulding above plinth.

Or,

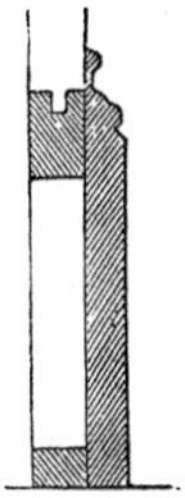

No. 267. Ditto. . . . . inch deal skirting; plinth 8 inches high, nailed to fillet and grooved grounds, and moulding above plinth, as drawing.

Or,

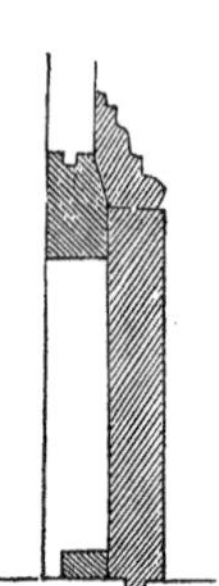

No. 268. Skirtings. . . . . inch deal skirting; plinth 10 inches high, grooved into floor boarding, nailed to fillet and to 1¼ grooved grounds, and moulding above plinth, as drawing.

Or,

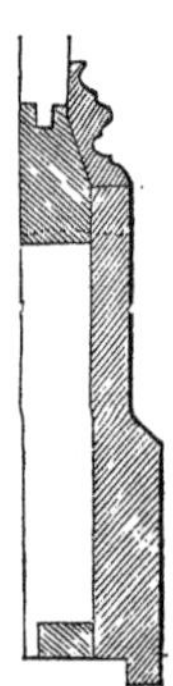

No. 269. Ditto. . . . . 1¼-inch deal skirting; plinth inches high, with ¼-inch sinking to form double face, grooved into floor, nailed to fillet and to 1¼ grooved grounds, and moulding above plinth, as drawing.

No. 270. Doors. The . . . . . to have { 1¼-inch or inch } { oak deal } door, formed with vertical ledges, rebated and beaded joints, nailed to three back braces, and hung with strong hook and twist hinges to solid rebated and beaded frame, 4″ × 3″, housed with iron shoe into step. Norfolk thumb-latch—wood stock lock.

No. 271. Ditto. The . . . . to have door formed of 2-inch { white pine Memel deal } stiles and top rail, filled in with inch deal battens, rebated and beaded joints, and backed with two horizontal (and, if necessary, two diagonal) braces framed into stiles, &c., the same hung with strong { hook and twist cross garnet wrought iron } hinges to solid Memel fir frame, rebated and twice beaded,

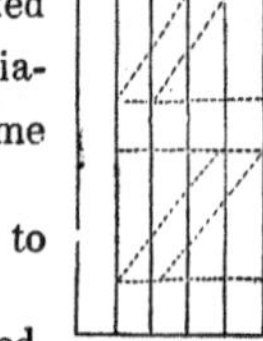

and housed with iron shoe into step. Norfolk thumb-latch to each door—fine plate 8-inch stock lock.

No. 272. Doors. Coach-house folding doors will be the same as the last described; rebated in their meeting stiles, hung with strong wrought iron hinges, and having bolts and swing bar.

No. 273. Ditto, common. The . . . . to have { 1-inch or / 1½-inch } yellow deal four-panel bead butt and square (or bead *flush* and square) doors, hung with cast iron butts to 1¼-inch jambs and heads; moulding on { one or / both } sides to cover the plaster joint; and iron rim brass-knobbed lock.

No. 274. Ditto, better. The . . . . to have 1½-inch yellow deal four-panel, ovolo and bead (*both* sides; or one side, and the other square) hung with iron butts in 1¼-inch single rebated jambs, with 2½-inch moulding on { one or / both } sides to cover plaster joint; and { mortise or / iron rim } brass-knobbed lock.

No. 275. Ditto, superior. The . . . . to have doors formed of inch panels, in 2-inch stiles and rails, ovolo and bead both sides (*one* side and square, in closets, &c.); hung with two 3½-inch best iron butts, in 1¼-inch jambs double rebated and beaded, and { 6-inch / 5-inch } moulded architrave on framed and splayed grounds. Good mortise lock with brass knobs to latch and bolt.

No. 276. Ditto, best. The . . . . to have doors formed of 1½-inch panels, having sunk margins ; or sinking in centre ; in 2-inch stiles and rails, the central stile being double and beaded up the middle, and the panels ogee and bead both sides. Door hung with the best 4-inch lifting brass or iron butts, in 1½ inch double rebated jambs, and 6-inch or 7-inch moulded architrave on framed and splayed grounds. Best mortise lock with . . . . . knobs to latch and bolt.

No. 277. Folding doors. The opening between . . . . rooms to have doors corresponding with the others in respect to their general character and mouldings, but hung folding, and having three panels in their height. Brass flush bolts top and bottom of one half, and the other furnished with mortise lock, &c., as other doors.

No. 278. Sliding doors. The opening between . . . . . rooms to have sliding doors, corresponding with the others in respect to their general character and mouldings, only that they will have an additional panel in height. The said doors to be hung by metal suspenders, to the axles of

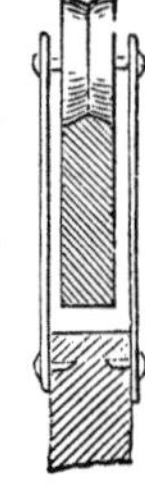

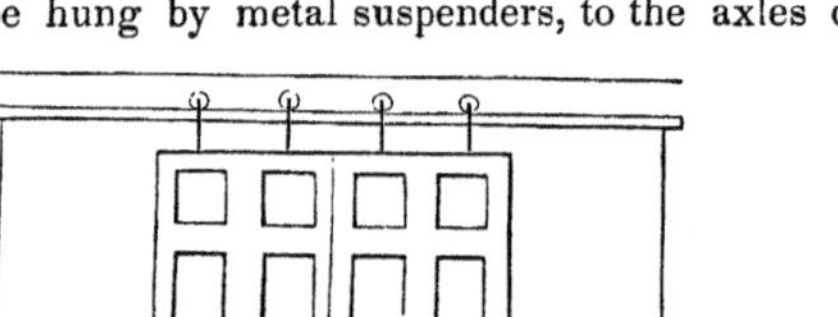

brass rollers, which will traverse a strong iron rail rod. The whole to be executed in the best manner, and conformable to the drawings.

No. 279. Outer doors. The door opening . . . . . . to be fitted with door formed of 1½-inch Memel deal ovolo bead and raised panels, three beads flush inside, in 2½-inch Memel stiles and rails.

hung with two strong 4½-inch butts to solid Memel fir frame, 4½″ × 3″, rebated and twice beaded, housed with iron shoe into step, with transome 4½″ × 3″, filled in with cast iron rebated frame-work for glazing, as drawing: best 10-inch iron rim brass-knobbed lock, having draw-back latch, barrel, and chain. Wooden architrave on the inside, as drawing.

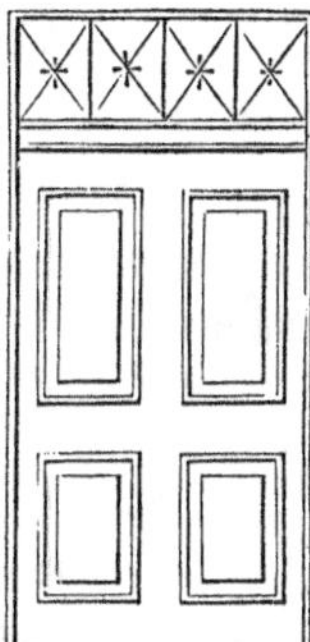

No. 280. ——— . . . . . . (as the foregoing, with this variation) "hung folding, with two strong 4½-inch butts to each half,"— "one half to have a 2-feet barrel bolt at top, and 12-inch ditto at bottom; the other a best 10-inch iron rim lock, &c., &c."

No. 281. Back doors. The door-opening . . . . . . to be fitted with door formed of 1½-inch Memel deal bead flush and square panels, in 2½-inch stiles and rails, hung with 4-inch butts in solid Memel fir frame, &c., &c., as No. 279.

No. 282. ——— . . . . as the foregoing, varying as No. 280 from No. 279.

No. 283. To either of the four foregoing doors, add "side lights to the said door, as drawing, having cast iron rebated lattice-work for glazing, set in solid fir frame, corresponding with the rest, with 2½″ panelled work below the lights."

No. 284. Door as the last, with *side*, but no *top* lights, and therefore no transome.

No. 285. If segment headed door, describe it, as drawing.

No. 286. If semicircular headed, describe it, as drawing.

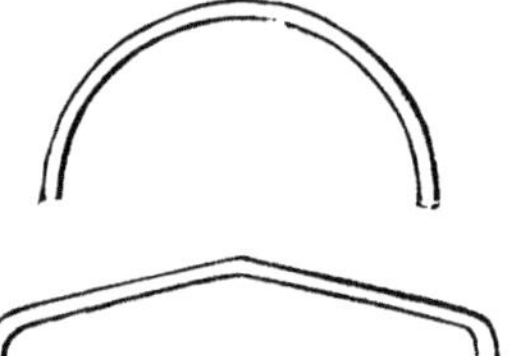

No. 287. If pointed arched, describe it, as drawing.

The top lights of the latter three may be termed fan-lights.

No. 288. If the doors be Gothic, the "ovolo and bead" or "ogee and bead" mouldings must be supplanted by "Gothic moulded, as drawings." It is impossible to specify for Gothic joinery, except as it regards the *substance* of the frames, transomes, stiles, and panels. Distinct drawings must be made for each particular case.

No. 289. Be careful that the general heading of "doors" include all dormer doors, trap doors, blank doors, &c. Doors to casings of water-closet pipes, cupboard and dwarf doors, sliding doors to buttery hatch, baized or cloth-covered doors, with self-closing spring hinges; whether to open one or both ways? whether panel-glazed, as A, or casement-glazed, as B? and whether any of the inner doors are to be prepared for *borrowed lights* above them.

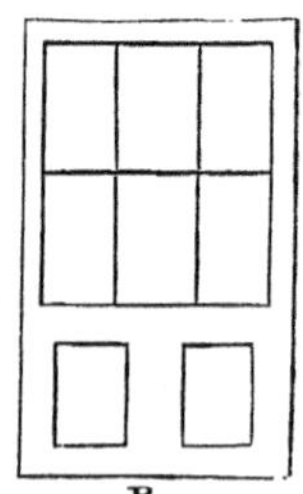

No. 290. Lantern-light. Lantern-light over the . . . . . , as drawings. Oak sill 6″ × 4″, rebated, sunk, weathered, throated, and grooved for lead. Angle standards of Memel deal 4″ × 4″, rebated and beaded; mullions 4″ × 3″, rebated and beaded; head ditto ditto. 2-inch Memel casements flush with the outside of frame (state if any are to open, and how ?). Inch Memel fascia board and moulding for lead covering. Raking board grooved into sill to cover plaster cornice, &c.

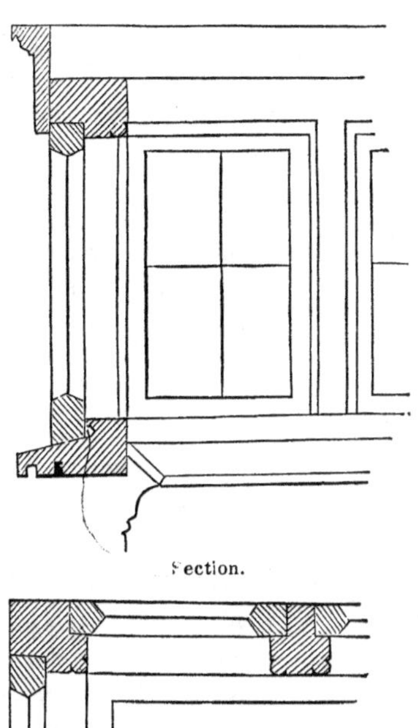

Section.

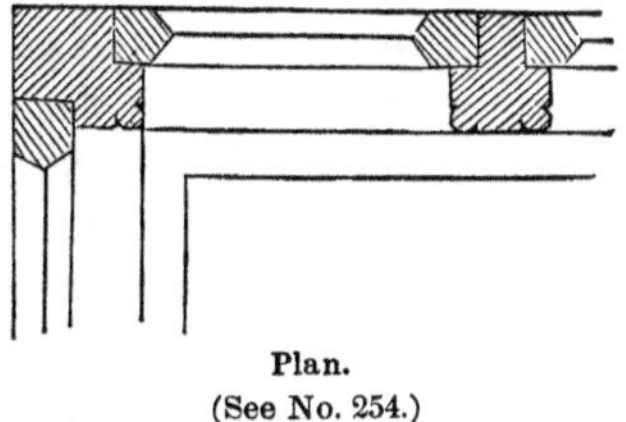

Plan.
(See No. 254.)

No. 291. As above, with segmental, semicircular, or arched pointed heads to the lights and frames, with spandril fillings, &c., as drawing.

No. 292. Windows, sash, simplest. The window-openings of . . . . . to have 2-inch or 2½-inch Memel deal sashes (double, or single, hung), with white lines, iron weights, and iron axle pulleys, in proper deal-cased frames, having oak double sunk sills 6″ × 3″. Good spring sash *fastenings*. Inch angle bead to plastered jambs and *soffits*; inch rounded ledge to cap the plastered back, and skirting of room carried round the recess.

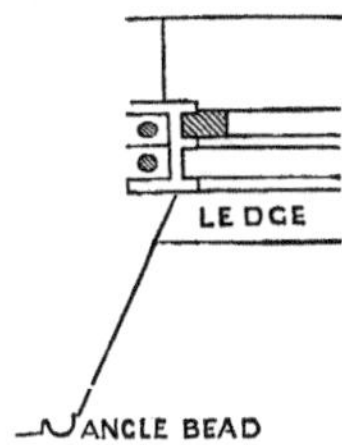

No. 293. Windows, sash, common. . . . . . same as foregoing to the word "*soffits*," continuing thus: inch deal back, moulded and panelled to match doors, and skirting carried home to the same.

No. 294. Ditto, better. . . . same as No. 292 to the words "*sash fastenings*," continuing thus: soffit, jambs, back, and elbows of inch deal, panelled and moulded to match doors, and moulding fixed on framed and beaded ground to form architrave.

No. 295. . . . . . . same as last, with the addition of the margin M, for Venetian blinds.

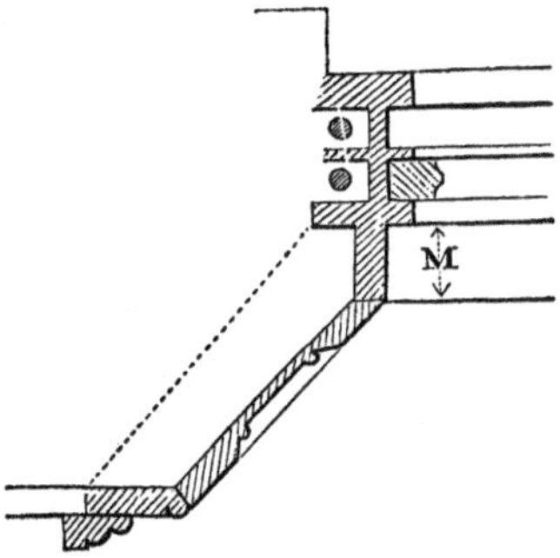

No. 296. Ditto, improved. Same as No. 292 to the words "*sash fastenings*," continuing thus: soffit, back, elbows, and properly hung folding shutters; the whole panelled and moulded to match doors, except the back flaps, which will be bead butt and *square*, to fall back against plastered jambs, in boxing formed by the grounds, and moulding fixed on the latter to form architraves as to doors. (Qy. if the addition No. 295?) See No. 298.

No. 297. Windows, sash, best. Same as last to the word "*square*," adding: to fall back against proper bead butt and square back linings forming boxing with the grounds, and architraves complete as to doors. (Qy. if the addition No. 295?) See No. 298.

No. 298. The shutters and back flaps to be properly hung with strong butt hinges; shutter latches, with furniture to match doors; and strong wrought iron locking bar.

No. 299. Same as No. 292 to the words "*sash fastenings*," continuing: additional cased frame for lifting shutters to be hung as the sashes, and to descend into a proper deal casing, as drawing, having hinged ledge at top. The shutters bead butt and square, with brass-headed iron screw in brass screw-hole, to fasten them, as shown by sketch. The front of shutter casing panelled as doors, and architrave also to match.

Section.

No. 300. Same as last, with the addition of soffit jambs and elbows, panelled as front of shutter casing.

No. 301. The window opening of . . . . to be fitted with 2-inch or 2½-inch } Memel deal sashes, in triple-light cased frame, as drawings; the central sashes double hung with best white lines, iron weights, and pulleys;—continuing to describe the rest of the inside joinery, as may be selected from Nos. 292 to 300 inclusive.

No. 302. If a *bow* window, describe it such. (See No. 305.)

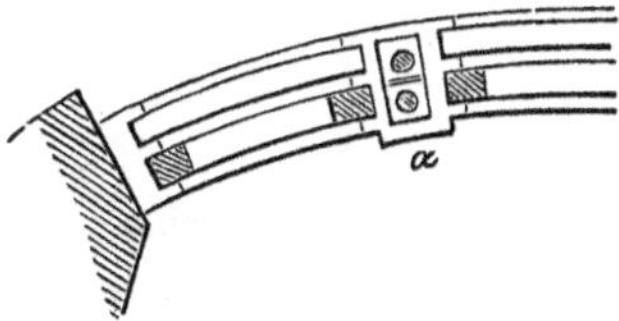

No. 303. If a *bay* window, say, "the openings of bay to be fitted with 2-inch or 2½-inch } Memel deal sashes, in proper cased frames," &c.,

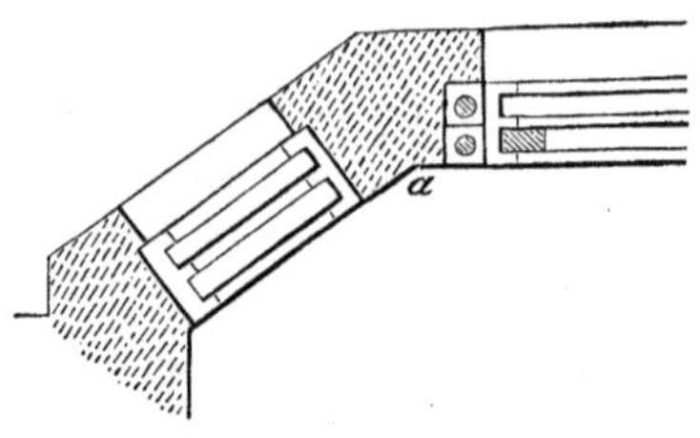

stating whether the central sashes only, or the whole of the sashes, are to be double hung, &c., &c. (See No. 305.)

No. 304. If a *Venetian* window, say, "the openings of Venetian window to be fitted," &c., &c., &c., as before. (See also No. 305.)

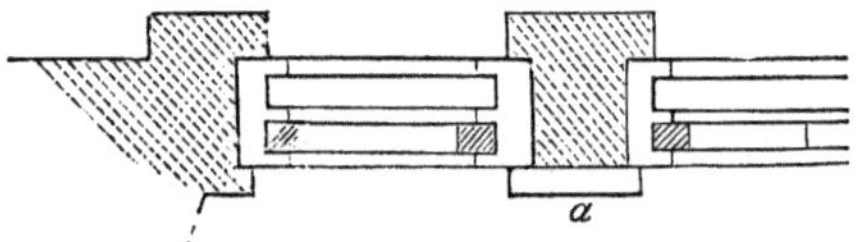

No. 305. The windows, Nos. 301 to 304, may have "wooden casing pilasters" at *a*, *a*, *a*, &c., which must be described "as shown in drawings."

No. 306. 307. 308. If the frames and sashes have "segment," "semicircular," or "pointed arched heads," describe "as drawings."

No. 309. Windows, casement. Fit up window-openings in . . with -inch deal casements, filled in with iron bars and lead (qy. diamond ?) work for glazing; (certain of them to be) hung with strong butt hinges, in solid fir, wrought, rebated, and beaded frames, and

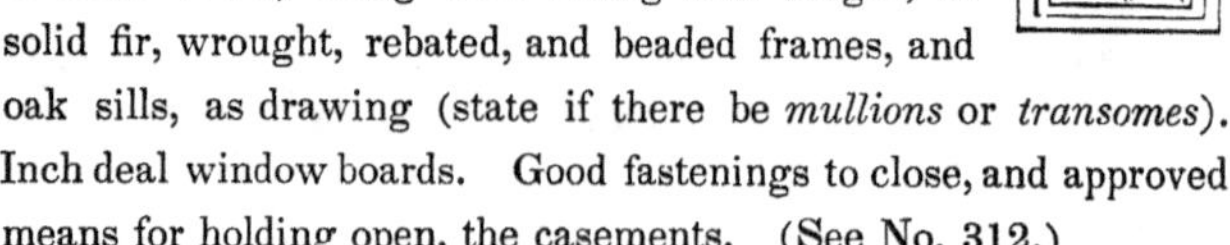

oak sills, as drawing (state if there be *mullions* or *transomes*). Inch deal window boards. Good fastenings to close, and approved means for holding open, the casements. (See No. 312.)

No. 310. Same as last, omitting "filled in with iron bars and lead for glazing." (See No. 312.)

No. 311. If inside shutters, soffits, backs, or elbows, select from No. 292 to 305. If outside shutters, make them conform with the doors described in Nos. 270 to 273, adding the required fastenings for securing them when open or shut.

No. 312. If the windows be Gothic, the casements will be described as hung in solid frames (mullions) (transomes) and oak sills, Gothic moulded, as drawings, with their hinges, bolts (top and bottom), latches, and fastenings, stating whether pointed headed, &c. Soffits, shutters, backs, elbows, &c., as from No. 292 to 305.

No. 313. The window openings of . . . to be fitted with 2-inch or 2½-inch Memel moulded and rebated casements, having vertical (and transverse ?) meeting stiles (and rails ?) as drawings. The same to be hung in solid Memel fir, wrought, rebated, and beaded frames 5″ × 3″ / 4″ × 3″ in oak double sunk sills, with strong 4-inch butts: good brass-knobbed latchet, and (brass bolts top and bottom of the opening casement) (or) patent rod-bolt to make the meeting casements, when closed, perfectly tight. For soffits, shutters, backs, elbows, pilasters, &c., &c., see Nos. 292 to 305.

No. 314. The windows of . . . . . to be fitted with . . . . . deal swing casements to hang on centres, as drawing, with apparatus for opening, closing, and fixing the same, in solid rebated and beaded frames and oak sills, as drawings.

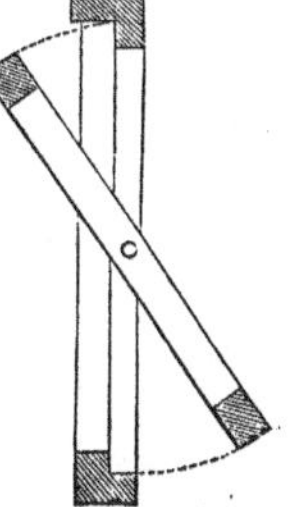

No. 315. *Note.*—Be careful that all common windows and doors, which have no fittings of joinery inside, be furnished with coin-beads, and that such windows have window-boards.

No. 316. Fit up the . . . . . . window-openings with neatly wrought luffer-boarding (state whether *fixed*,—or if it is to be made to close or open at pleasure, by each board revolving on a wood pin at each end), in solid Memel fir frame and oak sill. (If the boarding is to open and close, a rod and pegs, as sketch, must be made to revolve on pins in the head-piece and sill, with a handle, or other means for turning it.

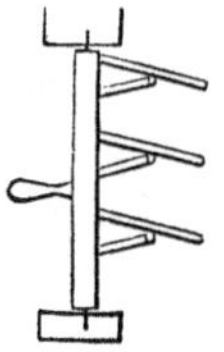

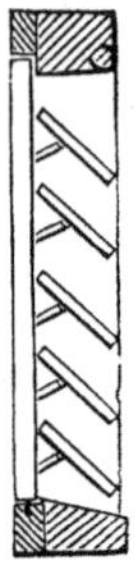

No. 317 Frame and fix a clock or bell-turret over the . . . . . ; the same to be of Memel fir, and agreeably to the drawings and the descriptions thereon.

No. 318. Stairs, common. The . . . . . . staircase to be fitted with inch deal steps having rounded nosings, on ¾-inch risers, framed into skirting and outer strings, with neatly turned newels and inch-square balusters, two on each step, and neat 2¼-inch rounded hand-rail. (See Nos. 321 and 322.)

No. 319. Stairs, better. The . . . . . staircase to be fitted with 1¼-inch deal steps, having moulded nosings, framed into skirting and outer string; the latter wrought, moulded, and capped, as drawing, with 1½-inch balusters; wainscot, hand-rail, and newels, cut and moulded as pattern. (See Nos. 321 and 322.)

No. 320. Stairs, best. The . . . . . staircase to be fitted with 1¼-inch deal steps, with moulded nosings along fronts and returns; inch deal risers; end-casing of steps cut as pattern, and fascia moulded as drawing; handsome curtail step, { wainscot / mahogany } hand-rail, and turned { wainscot / mahogany } balusters, two to each step. (See Nos. 321 and 322.)

No. 321. A sufficiency of cast iron balusters of corresponding pattern, to give stiffness to the hand-rail.

No. 322. The face of landing to have nosing and fascia corresponding with the steps and balusters also.

No. 323. The staircase of . . . . . to be fitted (as No. 319 or No. 320), adding, "and the soffit of stairs to be panelled with wood, as shown and described on drawings."

No. 324. The . . . . . staircase to be fitted with (as No. 319 or 320), adding, "and the space (or a certain part of it) under stairs to be inclosed with wood-panelled inclosure, moulded outside as drawings, and square on the inside."

No. 325. The staircase of . . . . . . to be (as No. 319 or No. 320), excepting that "cast iron ornamental balusters" will supersede the wooden ones.

No. 326. The . . . . to be approached by a flight of inch { oak / deal } treads framed into 1½-inch string bearers.

No. 327. Inclosures. Frame and fix at . . . . . . and . . . . . . , &c. { 1-inch / 1½-inch / 2-inch } { wainscot / deal } panelled inclosures, moulded or square, so as to correspond with the doors or other joinery with which they are seen or connected. (State whether there are to be skirtings or cornices, and if any borrowed lights therein.)

No. 328. Casings. Specify whatever *casings* (plain, panelled, or beaded) tnere may be, not before mentioned, such as to beams, lintels, bressummers' story-posts.

No. 329. Specify if any boarding (plain, grooved, tongued, and beaded, or otherwise) on battens against walls, or against quarter partitions; or whether any panelled casings against the same, as dados, or wainscoting; and whether base and surbase mouldings.

No. 330. The columns and pilasters in the . . . . . to be formed of 2-inch yellow deal staves, glued and blocked with turned yellow deal bases, and caps (if Tuscan or Doric). (If the caps are Corinthian or Ionic, they will be described as "carved according to the drawings.")

No. 331. Moulded architrave, &c., frieze, and glued, blocked, and moulded cornice (describe whether enriched, or with modillions, dentils, &c.)

No. 332. Describe all other carved work.

No. 333. Describe papier mâché in connexion with joinery. Where mouldings of panels, architraves, cornices, &c., &c., in the joinery, are to be *gilded*, they should always be enriched, and papier mâché is the best way of preparing for it. See published Book of Ornaments, and Tariff of Prices.

No. 334. Fit up the water-closet with -inch { deal / mahogany / cedar } pierced seat, and properly framed { (brass- / (iron- } hinged) flap of the same material, with moulded nosing to range with fixed sides, having boxed sinking for handle in one, and larger ditto ditto for paper in the other. Back and elbow beaded boards, 8 inches high, of same material as flap, &c. The riser to be of . . . . . . panelled, and casing for pipes, with doors, &c., as plan.

No. 335. Privies fitted with deal riser, seat, and cover, and back and elbow boards.

No. 336. Sundry fittings—as glass-washing troughs in butler's pantry, dish-washing ditto in scullery, and all such presses, shelvings, cupboards, &c., &c., as are positively connected with the permanent building; wooden chimney-pieces; rails and pins in closets, passages, and halls, &c., &c., &c.; fittings in butler's pantry, housekeeper's room, china closets, store rooms; knife and shoe, drying and brushing rooms; wash-houses, laundries, brew-houses, cook's closets, house-maid's closets, larders; salting-rooms, dairies, scalding-rooms, still-rooms, &c., &c.

No. 340. STABLES.—Miscellaneous Joinery; as Stall-posts 6 inches square, chamfered, with iron shoes; head-piece to match; stall divisions of -inch vertical oak boarding, ploughed and tongued joints, grooved into bottom rail 4″ × 3″, and into rounded top rail 4″ × 5″.—Racks ⅔ds width of stall, formed of rounded oak bars 1½ inch diameter, in rounded top rail 5″ × 4″, and bottom ditto 3″ × 3″.—Boxed oak mangers, occupying ⅓rd width of stall; standard post properly fixed in ground, with halter-pulley therein: the backs of stalls boarded as high as the stall divisions, and boarding round all the walls besides, ranging with the stall boarding.—Lockers for corn, &c. Traps for letting down hay.—Harness-room boarded top to bottom, with harness-pegs and saddle-trees, closets, &c.—Steps or ladders to loft.—Doors, windows, hay-loft doors, &c.—Ventilating trunks.—The loft-joists and boarding wrought fair where visible from below.—Trunk and apparatus for obtaining corn from the chest above. (See No. 344.)

No. 341. COACH-HOUSES.—Folding doors in jambs, heads, &c.—Story-posts.—Bressummer over . . . . door from saddle-room. (See No. 344.)

No. 342. Loose boxes boarded round as stables, with angular quadrant racks and mangers, of the same general character as to stalls. (See No. 344.)

No. 343. All required joinery to outhouses and coach gates, sheds, &c., cow-houses, piggeries, &c., &c. (See No. 344).

No. 344. The doors and windows suited to stables, coach-houses, outhouses, &c., will be found against Nos. 270, 271, 272, 273, 309, 310, 314, 315, 316; stable clock turret, 317.

No. 345 Final clause. The whole of the aforesaid joinery to be executed with sound and well seasoned timber, free from sap, shakes, and large or loose knots, and to be so early prepared that, after its fixing, it may remain secure from serious shrinkage. All obviously necessary or usually required ironmongery to be supplied and fixed by the Joiner, whether specified or not; and all hinges, locks, latches, bars, catches, bolts, &c., to be left perfect at the close of the works, easy in their action, and free from rust.

IRON AND METAL-WORK.

No. 346. The windows of . . . . (*i. e.* such as have no shutters, but where security by night is required) to be fortified by strong wrought iron bars, firmly screwed into the sills and heads.

No. 347. The windows and . . . . . of . . . . . (dairies and larders for instance) to be fitted with fly-wire instead of glazing;

Or,

The windows of . . . . . to have separate frames filled in with fly-wire, so that the glazed casements or sashes may open independent of them.

No. 348. Fix over the opening of . . . . . a sky-light of cast iron, or { zinc, or copper } formed as shown by drawing, the bars being of the section as sketch.

No. 349 Put to the fire-places of . . . . . wrought iron chimney-bar $2\frac{1}{2}'' \times \frac{1}{2}''$, properly corked at the ends.

No. 350. Qy. bolts to prevent brick hearth trimmers from spreading.

No. 351. Iron columns Provide and fix cast iron columns to support the . . . . ; the same to be of the best iron, cast hollow; the entire diameter being inches, and the thickness of the iron being not less than

$\frac{1}{5}$th of that entire diameter. Cast iron plate as drawing on the top.

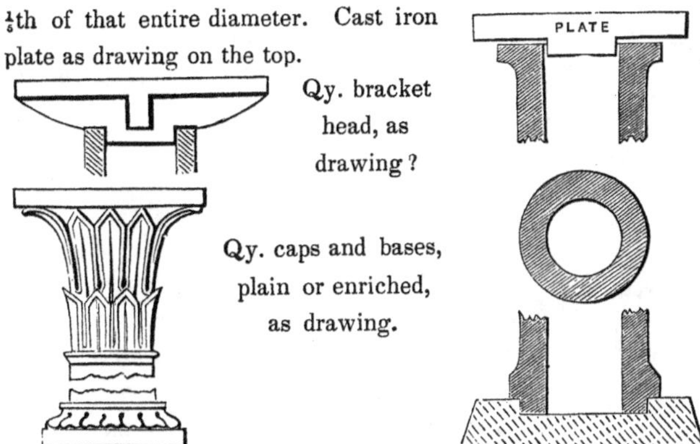

Qy. bracket head, as drawing?

Qy. caps and bases, plain or enriched, as drawing.

No. 352. Iron girders. Provide and fix cast iron girders over the . . . . ; the same to be of the best iron, of the form and full scantling (after shrinkage) shown in drawing.

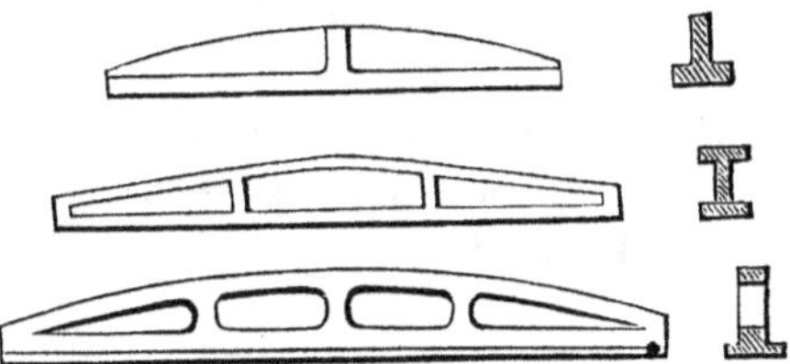

No. 353. Iron joists. Provide and fix cast iron joists (to receive either brick arches, stone floors, &c. ?); the same to be of the best iron, and of the full scantling (after cooling) shown by section.

No. 354. Sundries. Wrought iron tie-bolts? cast iron plates? chain bars.

No. 355. Iron roofs. Iron roofs can only be generally described as "of the best wrought and cast iron, and of the forms and full scantlings (after shrinkage) shown by the drawings," which cannot be too much detailed and described thereon. (See Bartholomew's Specifications, chap. 47.)

No. 356. Gutter cantilevers. Provide and fix . . . . . cast iron cantilevers to match with the wooden ones of . . . . . cornice; the same to be cast hollow to act as gutters in conveying the water from the gutter in front to the heads of water-pipes.

No. 356½ Shutes. Provide and fix along the eaves of . . . . . . roofs a cast iron gutter, as sketch, with proper bracket supports, &c.

Or,

Zinc shuting may be used.

No. 357. Water-pipes. Provide and fix the various cast iron water-pipes shown on plans; those of . . . . . to be of inches clear bore, those of . . . . . . of inches ditto, and those of . . . . . of inches ditto. All these pipes to have proper receiving heads, with roses or wire tops to prevent the descent of leaves or rubbish, and proper shoes at the bottom to turn off the wet from walls. The inside of pipes to be painted three times before fixing.

No. 358. Gratings. Provide and fix { wrought or cast } iron gratings over the areas of . . . . ; the same to open (single or folding) on centres, with means for securing the same when closed.

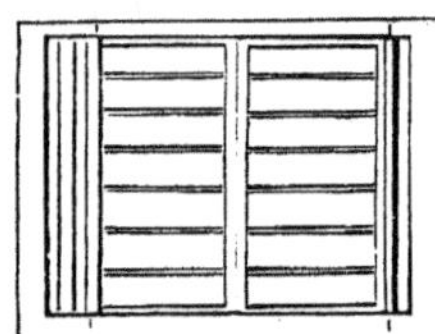

No. 359. Qy. any fixed gratings?

No 360. Provide and fix the various cast iron gratings to air-holes for ventilating under ground joists; also those required over cesspools, to the gutters or drains of . . . . ; also the several coal plates, with means for securing the latter inside, and iron stench traps.

No. 361. Rails and balusters, &c. Provide and fix the iron railing or palisading, wrought *plain* or cast *ornamental*, as indicated in plans, and shown in detailed drawing; also the rail and balusters, wrought *plain*, or cast *ornamental*, to the areas, landings, balconies, steps, stairs, &c., &c., the whole to be properly fixed, with screws, &c., in *wood*, or with lead running in *stone*-work, as the case may be.

No. 362. Gates. Provide and hang with proper wrought iron hinges, and centres (qy. revolving in brass cups?) the wickets or gates, single or folding, of wrought iron *plain*, or of cast iron *ornamental* shown in drawings; and with the bolts, stops, latches, locks, &c., thereon described.

No. 363. Iron doors. The opening into strong closet, plate closet, &c., to be fitted with an iron door and lock valued at £ .

No. 364. Wood and iron ditto. A good door may be formed by sheet iron panels, screwed and rebated into wrought iron stiles and rails, moulded in front and flush at back, the latter having fixed to them wooden stiles and rails to form panels like the front. The whole to be hung with strong 5-inch butts in iron rebated head and jambs; and brass lock on the iron side.

No. 365. Iron casement. The windows of . . . . to be fitted with cast iron casements, as fully shown and detailed on drawings. (The drawings will show the frames or outer rims, the meeting bars, the common bars, the part to open, and the means of opening and closing.) Whether the windows open, or only ventilators *in* them?

No. 366. Sundries to windows. If any particular bolts to make weather-tight the casements, or any metal slips to cover meeting joints of ditto, or to prevent water from passing over sill, describe them accurately; with any copper tubing that may be necessary to carry off wet or condensed moisture.

No. 367. Shutters. In Banking-houses, or other buildings where fire-proof security is required, Burnett's revolving shutters may be advantageously used.

No. 368. Provide and fix cast iron mangers and racks, as drawings, in stables.

No. 369.

No. 370

No. 371. General clause. Provide all the cast and wrought iron-work necessary to the completion of the Carpentry, according to common usage, whether herein specified or not, as spikes, nails, screws, holdfasts; also all cast and wrought iron or brass-work necessary to the doors, windows, shutters, lantern or sky-lights, and the joinery in general, as iron shoes to door-posts, hinges of the required varying description, locks ditto, latches ditto, bolts, bars, and chains ditto, and brass-knobbed handles.

Here proceed more minutely to describe the more important and particular Smith's work, as—

Wrought iron abutment king or queen-bolts, struts, straining-bars, and coupling-bolts, with their washers, nuts, and screws, to trussed beams or girders; wrought iron stirrups or straps and bolts, with their wedges, washers, nuts, and screws, to unite the king and queen posts and principals with the tie-beams of roofs. Cast iron shoes and cappings to wood story-posts.—Cast iron box, sockets, or casings, to receive the ends of girders, binders, or tie-beams.—Also any particular iron-work necessary to Stone-mason's work. All castings to be clean, sound, free from air-flaws, &c., and, in all importnt cases, as with columns and bearing-beams, thoroughly *proved* before fixing. All wrought iron to be thoroughly welded and hammered.

No. 372. Grates, stoves, ranges, &c. Provide grates for the various sitting and bed-rooms, of the following prices respectively, viz. . . . . . . The grates in the . . . rooms to have hobs.

Provide stoves for the . . . . , of the following descriptions and prices respectively, viz. . . . . . . Provide and superintend (including all carriage, men's time, and expenses) the fixing of a cooking apparatus and range for the kitchen, valued in themselves separately at £ . Fix smoke-jack of approved construction in kitchen flue. Qy. range or stove, or both, in back kitchen or scullery, valued at £ Hot-plates, &c. ?

Stove with oven, &c., valued at £ , in still-room. Scalding-stove in dairy scullery, valued at £ . Stoves and coppers in back kitchen or scullery, wash-house and bake-house, valued at £ . Ironing-stove in laundry, valued at £ . Arnott's stoves in . . . . and harness-room, valued at £ . . Qy. coppers and stoves in boiling-houses, brew-houses, &c.

No. 373. Bell hanging. Hang, on a proper board, painted and numbered, ... bells of varying tones, having springs and pendulums; the same to communicate, by means of copper wire passing through tinned or / copper } tubing (concealed in plastering), with . . . . . pulls, to be fixed where indicated on plans. The wires to be collected in the roof, and to be attached with the utmost care to a sufficiency of cranks and coil-springs. The pulls to be of the best suitable kinds, with knobs or lever-pulls, as here described. The pulls in . . . to be of . . . ; those in . . . . to be &c., &c.

PLUMBER'S WORK.

No. 374. Lantern top. Cover the roof over lantern with 6-lb. lead, to fold round and under the edge moulding on top of fascia.

No. 375. Ridges and hips. Cover the ridges and hips of roof or roofs with 7-lb / 6-lb lead 16 to / 20 } inches wide, securely fastened with lead-headed nails (and metal cramps if necessary), and closely dressed round ridge-roll and on to the slates.

No. 376. Dormers. Cover the (ridges and hips—or the tops) of dormer doors and windows with 6-lb. lead. If *ridges*, say "as to roof,"—if *tops*, say "as top of lantern,—or, if no lantern, describe the work similarly).

No. 377. Ditto. Qy. Cover the sides of dormer doors and windows with 5-lb lead.

No. 378 **Valleys.** Lay the valley gutters with 7-℔. lead, 18 inches wide, properly dressed under slates.

No. 379. **Chimney gutters.** Lay guttering at back of (and, in superior work, at sides of) chimney-stacks, of { 7-℔. / 6-℔. } lead, to turn up against the stacks, and properly dressed under slates.

No. 380. **Parapet gutters.** Lay the parapet gutters with { 8-℔. / 7-℔. } lead, to turn up { 7 / 6 / 5 } inches up the parapets, and to reach at least as high under slates. The gutter to have a medium width of inches, and 2-inch drips every feet, with a fall of not less than 2 inches in 10 feet.

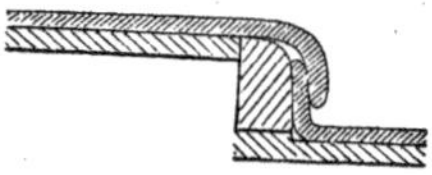

No. 381. **Flats.** Lay the flats (round lantern) and (elsewhere) with { 8-℔. / 7-℔. } lead, with all required roll joints, to turn up inches against walls, sill of lantern, &c., &c., and (where there is no vertical boundary) dressed round and under the edge moulding of eaves fascia. The lead to have a fall of 2 inches in 10 feet, and drips if required.

No. 382. Roofs covered with lead, described, as flats.

No. 383. **Flashings.** Flashings of 5℔. milled lead to be applied wherever the lead coverings of gutters, flats, or roofs, turn up against vertical masonry or wood-work. Said flashings to be chased into walls at least 3 inches, and be dressed down over the lead turn-ups at least 4 inches. It is often advisable to carry the flashing quite through the parapet.

No. 384. **Gutter cornices.** Line the gutters in eaves-wood cornices with 5-℔. lead (see Joiner) to fold over and under the front moulding, and turn up under slates two inches above the level of front moulding. Pieces of pipe with rose and boxing, to carry water from the gutter into the rain-water heads.

No. 385. Cisterns and troughs. Line the cisterns with lead, the bottoms of 8-℔. lead, and the sides of 6-℔. ditto; and line the troughs conducting through the roofs with 6-℔. lead.

No. 386. Laying on water, &c. Describe the pipes that may be necessary to conduct water into the cisterns from the town supply, the outer reservoir, or the force-pump in ground floor: also the waste-pipe required to prevent overflow, the dimensions thereof, the place into which it is to discharge, and any trap that may be required to prevent the ascent of effluvia from the drains below.

No. 387. Supply-pipes *from* cistern. Describe any pipes required to conduct water to the pans of water-closets, or to any other parts of the building, as washing places, baths, butler's pantries, or housemaid's closets; stating such as are to have brass cocks, &c.

No. 328. Water-closet. Provide and fix good and complete pan and apparatus to water-closet, with all required brass-pulls, levers, wires, cranks, copper ball-cocks, plugs, &c. Also soil-pipe, with trap to prevent the ascent of effluvia from the cess-pit or drain.

No. 389. Linings of troughs, &c. Line the washing trough in butler's pantry, or any other into which a pipe conducts from the cistern in roof; also bath (if of wood), &c., &c., &c., with lead of {6 or 5} ℔s. to the foot: each trough, &c., &c., to have a brass plug and chain, and pipe to conduct therefrom into drains. Where water is brought down to supply jugs, pitchers, or pails, a shallow trough should be supplied to catch the droppings, with pipe therefrom into drains or some movable vessel beneath.

No. 390. Pump. Provide and fix a (draw and) force-pump in the . . . . . . where shown on plan, with -inch pipe thereto from the (well, tank, or reservoir), and pipe therefrom into the cistern in roof.

No. 391. Sundries. Describe any sheet lead that may be required in the joints of masonry, or for the covering of any parts thereof; also any, necessary to cover the joinery, as the top of wood cornices, parapets, &c. All nails used in plumbers' work to be of copper.

Outhouses and inferior buildings will require lead-work, as flashings, &c., occasionally, though there may be no lead on their ridges, hips, &c. Bell and clock-turrets will be covered with lead in any circumstances.

No. 392. General clause. The lead-work to be laid and dressed down in the most careful manner, with as little soldering as may be, and with every regard to its expansion and contraction. The work to be left by the Contractor perfect and complete, without any cnarge for the labor, solder, nails, holdfasts, joints, &c., which may be necessary to the efficient completion of the works herein generally described and partially particularized.

GLAZIERS' WORK.

No. 393. Glaze the windows of the . . . . . with plate glass (or the upper sashes thereof with flatted glass and the lower with plate): the windows of the . . . . . with flatted glass (or the lower sashes thereof with flatted and the upper with best crown glass): the windows of the . . . . with best crown glass; the windows of the . . . . with glass of second quality; the windows of . . . . with third glass; the whole to be perfect in its kind, well puttied, and *left* perfect at the end of the works.

No. 393½. Rain-water pipes of cast iron [or copper], from eaves, gutters, &c., &c. Specify their position and bore, and describe them as having receiving heads and shoes to turn off the water from the walls.

PAINTERS' WORK.

No. 394. Paint the whole of the outside wood and iron-work { five or four } times in oil to finish a warm stone color, and the inside do. do. (which it is usual to paint) { four or three } times in oil to finish a warm stone color.

No. 306. Paint also, in like manner (here state the extra painting, as), the treads and risers of stairs of . . . . up to the stair-carpet rings: the floors, from the skirting to the carpet line; continuing to particularize all such sashes, frames, shutters, soffits, backs, elbows, doors, jamb and soffit linings, frames, skirtings, panelled inclosures and linings, as are to be finished with any particular color, or to be grained in imitation of some fancy wood and twice varnished. Finally, specify what *un*-painted joinery (as real wainscot, &c.) is to be twice varnished.

MISCELLANEOUS HINTS AND CAUTIONS

Union of new and old work.

In attaching any new work to a building, every allowance must be made for the sinking of the footings under pressure, and for the settlement of the masonry into itself. Thus, while it is necessary that a vertical groove, or indent, be made in the old work, to receive a corresponding piece of the new, it is still more essential that a freedom for the downward motion of the latter should be secured; otherwise, if it be tightly toothed and bonded into the old work, the result illustrated in the annexed sketch may be anticipated.

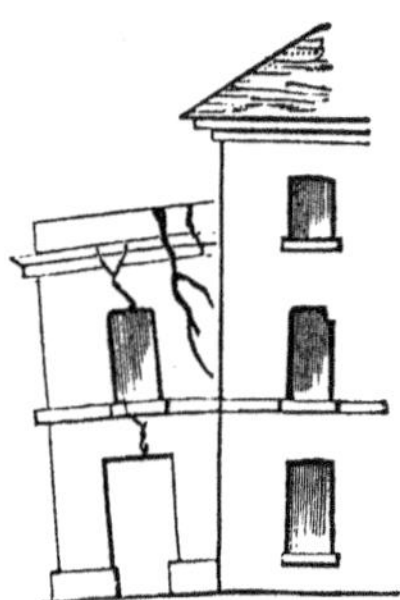

Union of ashlar facing with brick or rubble backing.

The same caution required in the latter must be here equally observed. The *backing* (composed of small material and much mortar) will settle more than the *face;* and the latter will consequently bulge. This is easily remedied by computing, and allowing for, the difference of settlement; and by a due regard to the occasional bonding of the ashlar, so as to make the wall *one* substance, instead of *two* differently conditioned. The preceding sketch illustrates the consequence of weight pressing upon unbounded ashlar and on yielding rubble.

Inverted arches.

Inverted arches must be used cautiously. Here is an instance, in which the points A and A were prevented by the inverted arch from sinking with the points B B, which latter sank the more from the pressure of the arch C in the direction of the dotted lines. It is not uncommon for the young Architect to *affect* precautionary *science*, without a due consideration of the peculiar circumstances of his case.

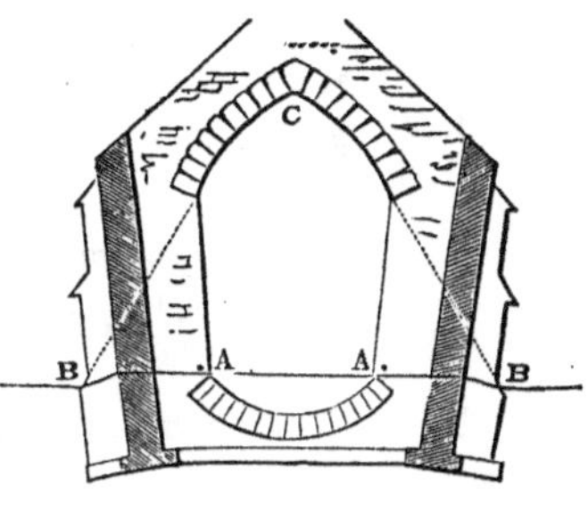

Drainage, &c.

Always endeavor, if possible, to get your water-closet cess-pit outside the building, so that it may be approached for cleansing without disturbing the interior. Be careful in the efficient use of dip-traps to prevent the ascent of rats from the outer sewer into the drains which are under the floors of the house. Rats are destructive in their operations, and if they die in the drain, prove, for a length of time, an unbearable nuisance. Drains may serve every purpose of carrying off soil and water; but the slightest opening in their upper part will allow the escape of effluvia into the space under the ground flooring, and thence into the rooms, unless that space be thoroughly ventilated with grated openings, allowing a thorough draught,—or, at least, a free ingress of fresh air and equal egress of foul. In the application of covered dry areas round the excavated basements of buildings, on no account omit their entire ventilation. If this be not attended to, the main walling, which they are intended to preserve from damp, may remain even more continually moist than if in immediate connexion with the natural ground. Moisture frequently rises up the walling from below its foundation, and, exuding from the face of the masonry, remains confined, unless it evaporate and escape. Without means to this end, a covered area will be merely a receptacle for damp, and may keep the masonry continually wet, even when the ground outside is perfectly dry. Be especially cautious that the water from the rain-pipes of the roofs and flats be not conducted by them into the foundations.

Fire openings

It will save much subsequent trouble and disturbance of masonry, to be assured as to the size and character of the stoves, grates, ranges, &c., which the proprietor will employ. In the kitchen and cooking-rooms, especially, precautionary care should be taken in suiting the openings to the intended apparatus. Do not forget to be prepared for a smoke-jack, &c.

Dwarf walls.

In constructing these, do not omit the holes, &c., necessary for under-floor ventilation.

Paving.

Be careful that the bottom, on which fine paving is laid, be dry and free from *staining* material. Common lime mortar is often injurious to pavements. Portland paving is especially liable to be disfigured by it.

Wrought stone-work.

In putting wrought stone-work together, *iron* is to be avoided as the certain cause of its subsequent destruction. The stone cornices, architraves, and dressings of many a noble mansion have been brought into premature ruin by the contraction and expansion of iron under the effects of cold and heat. But there are careless Contractors who will allow their Corinthian capitals and fluted shafts to be ruined, even before the entablature surmounts them ; and the young Architect will not, therefore, omit to insert a clause in his Specification (and to be peremptory in its enforcement), that all cut stone-work be securely preserved, during the progress of the building, with wood casing. It is surprising, how grossly indifferent each class of artificers is to the work of the others. It is still more surprising, to observe, how frequently they seem indifferent to the preservation of their own.

Slating.

Get rid of the Masons and Plasterers,—aye, and, as much as possible, of the Plumbers,—before your Slaters begin. The injury done to slating by the afterwork of chimney-tops, &c., is much to be dreaded. The cementitious " stopping" to a roof will not be efficiently done without close supervision: the ridge, hip, and valley courses will not be properly formed of large cut slates,—nor will every slate have its *two* nails, unless the Architect see to it.

Plastering.

Clear may be your Specification in forbidding salt sand, but, if your work be carried on in the vicinity of any estuary, the chances are (unless you be deemed cruelly strict), that the surface of your internal walls will vary with the weather, from damp to dry, like a sea weed, and throw out salt in such abundance that you may sweep off a cellar-full.

Beams, joists, and other timbers.—Lintels, bond, partitions.

It is the office of walls to carry beams, &c.; and that of beams to stay the walls from falling outwards or inwards; but it is the duty of Architects to see that the wood-work which supplants masonry, does not weaken the latter; *i. e.* that the ends of timbers inserted into walls may not, by compression or decay, leave the superincumbent masonry to loosen downwards. Thus, the beam A, though entering only a *portion* of the wall, presses upon the thorough-stone *e*, which throws the weight upon the *whole* wall,

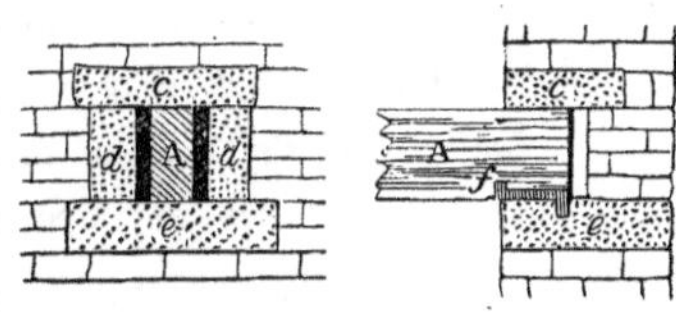

and has, by means of an iron plate *c*, a hold to secure its perpendicularity. The cover-stone C presses on the surface of the timber to confirm its security: but should the timber rot, the cover-stone will not sink, because sustained by the side-stones *d d*. To *prevent* rot, the backing and side-stones are left free of the timber, so that air may traverse round it. The habit of placing the ends of beams on a template, as G, is bad. The only justification of the employment of wood, so built into the walls, is when it forms a continuous plate, that it may act as a bond to preserve the perfect horizontal level of joists, which, however, should extend a little beyond the plate, so as to have a bearing also on the

G

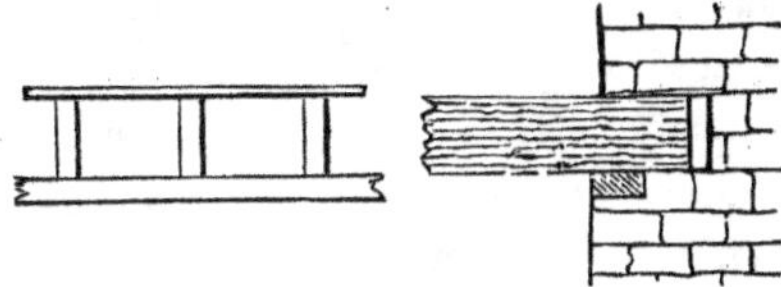

solid of the wall. Careful inspection will then so manage the construction of the wall in this part, as to leave it but little weakened by the air hollows required for the plate and joists; unless, indeed, it be very thin,—as only one brick, for instance,—

Beams, joists, and other timbers.—Lintels, bond, partitions.

when no law of common sense can justify the use of continuous bond. Where joists uninterruptedly cross a thin wall, which is to support another story of masonry, let there only be one plate, thin and on its edge, in the centre of the wall, so that at least a brick on edge may be placed on each side of it, to fill up the intervals between the joists, and give solid support to the superincumbent masonry. On no account let the upper part of the wall be separated from the lower by a mere layer of perishable wood, or supported by a range of joists on their edge. It has often occurred to us that iron hooping should be more used than it is as the internal bonding of walls. At the same time, it must be remembered, that bond timbering is necessary, at intervals, to receive the nails of the battening. When, however, the wall is thin, it may be imperative to avoid its use, employing old oak bats for that purpose. In short, let it be the care of the young Architect, so to contrive the union of his masonry and carpentry, as that the entire removal of the latter may leave the former secure in its own strength. In the use of *lintels* especially, he should be cautious. They are useful as bonds to unite the tops of piers, and as means for the fixing of the joinery; but they ought never to be trusted to as a lasting support of masonry,—that support being always really afforded by the relieving segment arch above the lintel. We are aware, that a bressummer may be termed a large lintel; and that, here, at least, the support of the masonry is truly intended. The use of the bressummer, in shop-front openings, is an evil necessity to which we must often submit; and all that an Architect can do, is to make the best of a bad job, by *wrought* iron trussing, which will at least give adequate *strength*, though it may not insure permanent durability. If *time* spare it, *fire* may destroy it; and the latter evil is not to be met even by iron, which, if wrought, will bend, —if cast, will crack, with heat. Let the arch, then, or some modification of it, be always used—if possible.

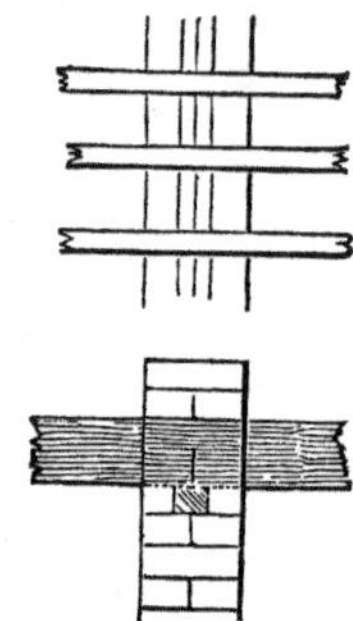

Partitions of wood should not be left to the sagacity of the Carpenter. Under all circumstances where they have to support themselves over voids, or to bear, or participate in the bearing of

Beams, joists, and other timbers.—Lintels, bond, partitions.

a pressure from above, they should be considered by the Architect in his Specification, and carefully studied in making the working drawings. It is not enough merely to say, that "they are to be trussed so as to prevent any injury to ceilings by their own pressure, or that of the roof above them;"—marginal sketches should be made, showing the disposition of the skeleton framing, with whatever iron-work is necessary to its security. See, for instance, what a Carpenter may do, unless well directed: a roof C, bearing partly on the partition A, when it should have borne only on the walls; and, instead of distressing the partition, should have rather held it suspended: the partition A bearing down with its own weight, and that of the roof, on the floor B, instead of being so truss-framed in its length as to leave the floor unconscious of its existence. We presume no ignorance in the young Architect as to the manner of doing these things; and only call on him not to suppose they are so obvious as to be done without his guidance.

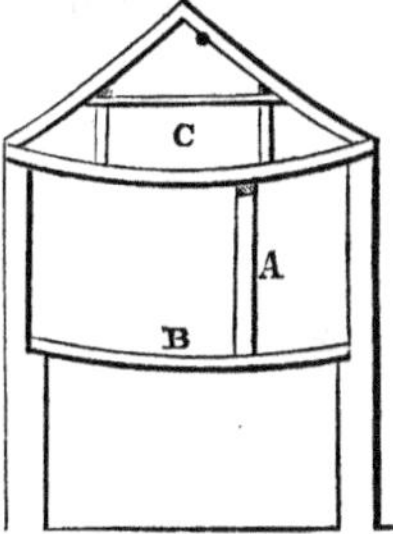

In the framing of roofs, give a maximum strength to the purlins: the undulating surface of a weakly-purlined roof will soon proclaim its defect in this particular. The position of the principals should not be observable from without.

Floors; simple and framed, &c.

For permanent and uniform strength, there is no floor so good as one composed of simple joists, stiffened by cross bonding; but, in very large rooms, there is more economy in the compound floor of binders and joists, or of joists, binders, and girders. There may be particular reasons for girders, &c.; as, when the weight of the floor has to be thrown upon piers, and not on a continuous wall of uniform strength; but the usual motive to the use of the compound floor, in rooms which exceed 18 or 20 feet in width, is a legitimate economy of materials. It is only necessary to caution the young practitioner on the necessity of

Floors; simple and framed, &c.

considering, that girders have to perform the duty of cross walls; that they should be trussed to prevent their "sagging" even with their own weight; that their scantling should allow for the weakening effect of the cuttings made into their substance to receive the timbers they support; that their trusses should be wholly of *iron* (and not partially of oak, for the Author has seen the bad effects of the shrinkage of oak struts); and, especially, that the end of each girder, instead of being notched on perishable templates of wood, and close surrounded with mortar and masonry, should be housed in a cavity (as we have already described) with an iron holding plate; or inserted into a cast iron boxing, notched into a thorough-stone, leaving a space (however small) for air to circulate about it, and prevent rot. The failure of a girder involves the failure of all the rest of the floor; and, though *all* timbers inserted in masonry should have a more careful regard to their preservation from decay than it is usual to bestow, it will be readily admitted, that too much care cannot be given to those leading bearing timbers, without the permanent duration of which the durability of the large remainder is of no avail.

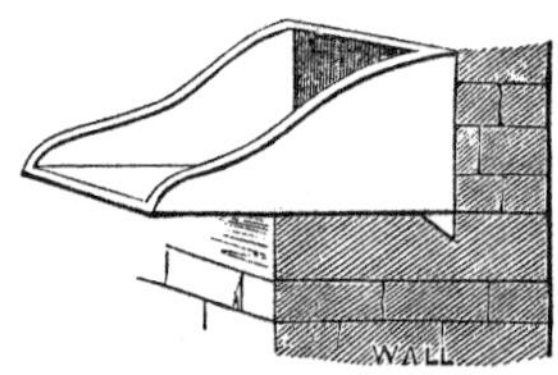

Roofs.

The same remarks applying to the extremities of girders apply also to tie-beams.

Ceilings.

To procure a good ceiling in single-joist floors, it is necessary there should be ceiling joists crossing below the others: and it is a question whether the ceiling joists, under double-framed floors, instead of being chase-mortised *into* the binders, should not be in unbroken lengths nailed *under* the binders. Where the ceiling joists (as under roofs) are likely to be trodden upon, they must be well secured.

Sound boarding.

Always consider whether the occupants of any particular room will be annoyed by the noises of the rooms below or above. Sound boarding and pugging considerably increase the weight of the floor, the scantling of whose timbers should therefore be thought upon. Water-closet partitions should be well pugged.

Mice in partitions and skirtings.

The space behind the skirtings is often a thoroughfare for mice, which also contrive to travel from floor to floor in the hollows of the quarter-partitions, and become in several ways a great nuisance. Plaster or wood stopping is not always so efficacious as the use of broken glass in those secret passages which they are prone to frequent.

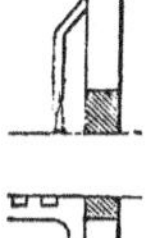

Coverings to gutters, cisterns, &c.

The liability of gutters and cisterns to become choked with snow, or infested with leaves, &c., renders it advisable to protect them with a boarded covering, which may preserve the under current of water from receiving what may speedily produce a chokage or overflow.

Iron columns, beams, &c.

On this most important subject we say but little, that we may signify the more. Here, the young Architect should not move a step without carefully consulting the experienced knowledge of the Engineer. Tredgold's "Practical Essay on the Strength of Cast Iron" should be well studied, whenever necessity compels the support of heavy and loaded superstructures by iron columns and beams. A careful computation of the weight of the mere building, added to that of its possible burden, with allowance for theoretical fallacy, and a due estimate of the increased strength of the hollow pillar, as compared with a solid one having the same amount of metal, must be made, examined, and re-examined, before the Specification be issued.

www.ingramcontent.com/pod-product-compliance
Lightning Source LLC
LaVergne TN
LVHW011209110826
845150LV00006B/1377

* 9 7 8 1 4 2 5 5 1 7 6 0 1 *